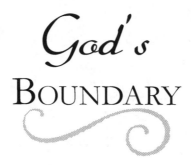

God's BOUNDARY

Sunday Okoh

WestBow
PRESS
A DIVISION OF THOMAS NELSON

WestBow Press books may be ordered through booksellers or by contacting:

WestBow Press
A Division of Thomas Nelson
1663 Liberty Drive
Bloomington, IN 47403
www.westbowpress.com
1-(866) 928-1240

ISBN: 978-1-4497-8704-2 (sc)

Library of Congress Control Number: 2013903853

Scripture taken from the King James Version of the Bible.

Printed in the United States of America

WestBow Press rev. date: 3/18/2013

Also by Sunday Okoh: Add Patience, The Grace of God and Without Offence.

God's Boundary
Sunday Okoh
Manuscript edited by Dr. Jonah Amodu
Everlasting Foundation Ministries International
P.O. Box 1105, Zaria, Kaduna State, Nigeria.
E-mail: sunnyo_eve2@yahoo.co.uk
Phone: +2348034533203
Website: www.efmin.org

Unless otherwise stated, all Scripture quotations are from the King James Version of the Bible.

Table of Contents

Dedication

To my darling wife, Evelyn Okoh.

There will always be casualties in the race of life if our focus shifts from the main goal, which is Jesus.

Acknowledgements

UNTO THE KING IMMORTAL, THE ONLY wise God be all the glory and honour for His call upon my life that has changed me completely.

Can I ever thank my parents in the Lord, Rt. Rev. (Dr.) David and Pastor (Mrs.) Bakare enough for all their impartations in my life? I am forever grateful.

Jointly, with all the Pastors in JAWOM we have had opportunity to serve the Lord. And our labour together has been as a result of our 'sitting together' in heavenly places. I appreciate our joint work for kingdom expansion and the individual personalities of JAWOM Pastors that have impacted my life.

The Council and Membership of JAWOM Solution Centre, GRA Zaria has been so much encouragement for my ministry work in the Centre. I am appreciative of the honour of being a pastor to such a congregation of God's people. You are simply the best!

My Pastors and family friends, Pastor (Dr.) and Dns. Folorunsho who recently obeyed the Lord's call to a foreign land, are highly appreciated for their blessings in our lives as a family. Their children are not left out in this appreciation.

In am thankful for the efforts that Dr. Jonah Amodu, who is a personal friend of many years, put to the editing of this work. Sis. Francisca Oche who spent so much time in the typesetting of this book is hereby acknowledged.

My biological parents, Mr. and Mrs. Okoh, whose coming together in marriage several years ago set the stage for my birth, is highly appreciated. The impact of my siblings on my life as we grew up together is very much appreciated. Shouldn't I thank my parents in-law, Mr. and Mrs. Eyegbagharen for giving me their daughter in marriage? I say a 'big thank you' to them.

At a time that I had a break in my book publication ministry, some people showed concern. Two of them are worthy of mention here: Dns. Kemi Igbadun and Mrs. Josephine Bako who asked me about other publications. I guess some people prayed secretly for me to pick up my book publication work again. To all such I say a big thank you. God has finally answered their prayers with the coming of this book.

Last, but certainly not the least, the role that my wife played in getting this work out is immeasurable. Thank you dear.

Introduction

In Genesis, the first book of the Bible is the story of creation. It is on record that God created the whole universe in just six days. One interesting thing that happened in the creation story was that God did not leave man to find his bearing on earth, but He planted a garden for man's comfort. In the Garden of Eden where God planted the man, He gave man a commandment not to eat of the tree of the knowledge of good and evil. When the all-wise God restricted Adam from eating of that particular tree, God was simply setting a boundary for man. Little did Adam know that the boundary was for his good. The day that the devil deceived him to go beyond God's boundary, he met his waterloo.

There is always a temptation to step out of God's boundary set for us in His word. But when we muster courage to resist such temptation, we set up ourselves for a blessing. Every scriptural injunction is for our good. God will still remain God whether His instructions are kept or not. When Adam disobeyed the word of God by eating of the forbidden fruit, God did not diminish in His glory and splendour. But Adam lost out of the garden. Every act of disobedience excludes you from the garden of God's goodness.

Our loving, Heavenly Father is concerned about our ultimate happiness and will not put anything in place that will hurt us. His laws as enshrined in the Bible are meant to guide us in the best pathway for our lives.

This book, 'God's Boundary' came as an inspiration from God. At a time when I began to wonder about the happenings around, both in the Church and in the world, it occurred to me that people are bent at pushing the boundary that God has set for humanity, for the sake of freedom to live for pleasure.

Over a period of approximately three months, I was helped of the Holy Ghost to prayerfully put together Biblical treasures that can guarantee the believers' stay within God' boundary. The next twelve chapters of this master piece, guarantees contact with the wisdom and the power of God to live distinct in a world that is fast eroding in ethical values and in the fear of God. Happy reading!

Chapter One

A Good Conscience

"Holding faith, and a good conscience; which some having put away concerning faith have made shipwreck" 1 Tim. 1: 19.

CONSCIENCE IS SIMPLY THE VOICE OF God in man. It is an integral part of human nature and it is supposed to be active in every being. When Adam and Eve tasted the forbidden fruit, they felt ashamed and attempted to hide themselves from God (Genesis 3: 7-10). It was their conscience that convicted them of their nakedness. When David had the opportunity to kill Saul, he did not do so. Rather than kill Saul, he cuts off the skirt of Saul's robe privately. As soon as he did that, the Bible records: *"... David's heart smote him, because he had cut off Saul's skirt"* 1 Sam. 24: 5. His conscience pricked him because he was not supposed to touch God's anointed.

The gift of a good conscience is God's way of keeping us within His boundary. I like to say categorically

1

that, there is no greater mentor that exists than the conscience of man: it teaches us to choose between good and evil especially when it is alive and active.

The story was told of a poor woman who went to a store and stole an item successfully. On her way home, a disturbing feeling gnawed at her peace of mind. She had to return to the store and placed back the stolen item, after which she returned home feeling relieved. The conscience does a lot of good when a man works according to its dictates.

When Paul was writing to Timothy in the book of 1 Tim. 1: 19, he alluded to the fact that some people could actually put away their conscience. Of course the consequence is what he called "a shipwreck of the faith".

The Law Sensitizes Our Conscience

Conscience can be viewed as the law of God inscribed in the hearts of men. Due to the fact that the conscience of man can be ignored or suppressed, the need for the written law came into existence in God's dealing with His people, Israel.

The Ten Commandments were given to Israel by God to sensitize their conscience. The law is actually not meant for the man that has good conscience, but rather for the man that has either ignored or suppressed his conscience.

"Knowing this, that the law is not made for a righteous man, but for the lawless and disobedient, for the ungodly and for sinners, for unholy and profane, for murderers of fathers and murderers of mothers, for manslayers, for whoremongers, for them that defile themselves with mankind, for menstealers, for liars, for perjured persons, and if there be any other thing that is contrary to sound doctrine" 1 Tim. 1: 9-10.

In every nation for example, there are laws that govern its people. When the people obey the laws of their land, they are more likely to live in peace and be stable as a nation. But when people refuse the law, anarchy sets in. The rule of law in a country is a step in the direction of peace and tranquility. It is actually a people that are against the laws of a land that are called rebels. And rebels are supposed to face the full wrath of the law.

Unfortunately however, some laws in some nations are made by a people without an active conscience. When such happens, the law becomes a license for their evil practice. You can be sure if homosexuals are the bulk of the law makers in a given society, they will make laws that will suit their homosexuality. A senator in Nigeria once canvassed for the legalization of prostitution and the suspicion was that, "he could be a potential customer".

A 'conscienceless' society is highly endemic to lawlessness and will work towards breaking the limits of morality. And a wise man once said, "He that loses his conscience has nothing left that is worth keeping".

God's Wrath for 'No Conscience'

When people live their lives without conscience, they set up themselves for God's wrath.

"The wrath of God is being revealed from heaven against all the godlessness and wickedness of men who suppress the truth in their wickedness" Rom. 1: 18 NIV.

There is no such person as a wicked man who has his conscience intact. This is true because the loss of a man's conscience is the beginning of wickedness. I recently read the story of a 34 year old young man who butchered his 57 year old mother and buried her in a well inside the compound where they live. What could have led to such wickedness if not a lack of conscience?

Much of the good that the world has seen was borne out of a good conscience and much of the evil that has happened to the world came out of an evil conscience. With all optimism, conscience is at the centre of people's behaviour as to what, when and how they act.

One of the manifestations of an evil conscience is the suppression of the truth. Of course, when the truth is suppressed in any given society, such a society goes under the flood gates of hell. The suppression of truth could be rightly labeled as corruption. And it could be catastrophic when corruption takes hold of a people. Surprisingly, corruption may not only be a property of political leaders but of spiritual leaders as well.

Some pastors are so corrupt that they could even sleep with their Church members in the process of deliverance. Such a practice is a manifestation of a suppressed conscience. A pastor without conscience is like a moving trailer without breaks: he will soon clear his members out of the way of righteousness. When the two sons of Eli, Hophni and Phinehas defiled the altar, it attracted the wrath of God (1 Samuel 2: 12-34). Both under Heaven and in the world to come, no wickedness will go unpunished.

The Devil's Strategy

Often times, the devil does not come against people in every body's glare, he rather comes subtly. That is why some don't believe in the existence of the devil. While his works are manifest, he tries to remain faceless. As Christians, we are not supposed to be ignorant of the devices of the devil. One of the ways that he operates is by thwarting or suppressing the conscience of man. If he succeeds in this, he appears innocent while evil is being perpetrated.

If you are familiar with the operations of the devil, you will note that when Jesus was born, the devil was not happy. So, when the story of His birth was narrated by the wise men to Herod, the devil entered Herod, suppressed his conscience and gave him license to kill all children under the age of two years, without any ill feeling (Matt. 2: 1-18).

For the sake of one man, Herod brought untold pain to several people. In the same vein, all the bombings, heartless killings and acts of terrorism that we see in the world today, are a result of a suppressed conscience by the devil. Unfortunately, in the counter terrorism war, the world doesn't seem to be looking the way of the devil. Do you see how clever the devil is? The devil prefers to give terrorism religious label so that he could absolve himself from it. Of course, it is wrong for any religion to disregard the sanctity of the human life under any guise. I believe that a good civilization should be knowledge driven, love motivated and conscience sensitized.

Sometimes ago, I had an understanding of what happened when the devil realized that he had made a mistake in crucifying the Lord of glory. While Jesus was on the cross, it spelt doom for the kingdom of darkness. The devil realized rather too late that trouble looms for him, so he did something desperate. He entered some people that passed by and inspired them to tempt the Saviour in the old fashioned way: "...*If thou be the Son of God, come down from the cross*" Matt. 27: 40. That is the devil trying to truncate the redemption process! Do you remember his language in Matt. 4: 3? "...*If thou be the Son of God, command that these stones be made bread*". In verse 6 "...*If thou be the Son of God, cast thyself down....*" Can you see that? The same old language of Matthew chapter four was used again in an attempt to bring Jesus down from the cross in Matthew chapter twenty seven verses forty. The devil has not changed his language; he has only changed tactics by trying to hide his identity! In an attempt to hide his identity, the devil uses man by suppressing his conscience.

The Inner Peace

According to John Chrysostoma, "Not fame and wealth, not great power and physical strength, not a magnificent table and elegant clothing, not any other human advantage can bring true happiness. This comes only from spiritual health and a clear conscience". When the conscience is obeyed, the soul is at rest. That is indeed the secret of peace.

Quite recently, my wife requested that I should buy some vegetables on my way home from an outing. When I got to the place where I was to buy the vegetables, there were a number of people that the woman was attending to. I brought out money and made my request for the vegetables. By the time she gave me the vegetables, I was confused as to whether I had paid her for it or not. She felt I had given her the money and she allowed me to go. But on my way home, I had restlessness in my spirit. I went back to her and asked her to check very well if I had paid, but she couldn't really confirm it. So I made a payment not minding if I had paid earlier or not. Then, my spirit had rest. In all probability, the restlessness I had in my spirit could be a pointer to the fact that the payment was not made in the first instance. Even if it was made, wisdom demands that I attend to the voice of conscience.

A wicked man is one who has jettisoned his conscience and is given to all manner of evil. To such a one, the Bible declares clearly: *"There is no peace, saith the LORD, unto the wicked"* Isaiah 48: 22.

Wickedness is a terrible lifestyle that devoid a man of inner peace. The Bible affirms, *"The wicked run away when no one is chasing them..."* Prov. 28: 1 NLT. What then will be chasing a wicked man when no one is behind? It must be his conscience!

The way out of this kind of a miserable life is repentance. Only in true repentance is the restlessness of the sinful soul assuaged. When a sinner approaches God in true repentance, asking God for His mercy and surrenders his life to Christ completely, the first sign of forgiveness he senses in his spirit is peace like a calm ocean. This is because when the sinful soul recognizes God's forgiveness, it clears the conscience of guilt. It appears to me as if this is the highest operation in the human soul that is beyond logic.

Apart from the gift of life, the most important gift that God has given to the fallen man is the gift of salvation. Any man who has not received this gift is simply boxing a shadow and will live in misery, until he gets it.

Part of what happens to man at salvation (when he gives his life to Christ) is the renaissance of a clear conscience. And, a clear conscience is a well spring of life bubbling unto undeniable peace!

Restitution

When some of us gave our lives to Christ in those days, one of the popular teachings at that time was the issue of restitution. We were requested to return stolen items and make amends where we wronged people. I remember very clearly, one of the things I did those days was to visit a public library where I had borrowed permanently, a novel which I fell in love with. As at that time, the book was no more in my possession but I still went to tell the authorities to hold me responsible for the novel. They cleared me and that gave me a conscience devoid of guilt.

When Zacchaeus had an encounter with Jesus in Luke 19:1-10, without being told, Zacchaeus promised to return every stolen item.

"And Zacchaeus stood, and said unto the Lord; Behold, Lord, the half of my goods I give to the poor; and if I have taken anything from any man by false accusation, I restore him fourfold" vs 8.

This act of making amends where possible is what is called restitution. It does not mean it must be a fourfold restoration as promised by the over-zealous Zacchaeus. It simply means make amends where necessary and possible.

Even though this act looks old-fashioned in the body of Christ, it does the conscience a lot of good when practiced. This is important especially where stolen properties are involved. It is not morally correct for example, that a robber who stole valuables comes to give his life to Christ and continues to enjoy the loot from his robbery. For conscience sake, let that robber who has turned over to Christ forget the pleasure of his robbery. The lesson from the story of Zacchaeus and his encounter with Jesus was that, he was not rebuffed by the Master when he promised to carry out restitution.

Remember

"The conscience should not be evaded, since it tells us inwardly how to live in conformity to God's will, and by severely censuring the soul when the mind has been infected by sins, and by admonishing the erring heart to repent, it provides welcome counsel as to how our defective state can be cured" - St. Philopheos of Sinai

"The disease of an evil conscience is beyond the practice of all the physicians in the world" - Gladstone.

There is a fountain flowing, drawn from Emmanuel's vein, when sinners plunge beneath the flood, they loose all their guilty conscience.

Chapter Two

The Power of Contentment

I BELIEVE IN STRONG TERMS, THAT one of the things that can keep us within the limits of God's boundary is contentment.

Contentment does not mean accepting just anything that comes your way. Rather, it is the acceptance of God's provision for your life per time. The Bible has something to say about contentment: *"But godliness with contentment is great gain"* 1 Tim. 6: 6. There is no godly person who has contentment that does not have great gain.

In the secular world, gain is the driving force of every business. Unfortunately, the quest for gain has taken godliness away from many. This accounts for why people use several unjust measures to keep being in business. We have heard so much of counterfeit drugs that governments around the world have been trying hard to curtail. The insatiable desire for gain is a prime factor for these anomalies. It is wickedness to consider gain above life in any business endeavour. Why should you do a business that jeopardizes human life just because of money?

Great Gain

The crave of the world today is their desire for much gain, but they forget that there is something better. The Bible calls it "Great gain." God is not just interested in our gain; He is interested in our great gain. It is great gain when you make money in a godly way. When you render a service to humanity and you get paid for it, it is called great gain. The gain is great because it is two-dimensional: the society benefits from it and you benefit also. The first consideration in the gain that could be termed great is the larger society. It is actually fraudulent for a man to receive something for nothing.

When a believer commits himself to being a blessing, he sets himself up for a great gain. The essence of living is to be a blessing. This understanding delivers a man from covetousness. And of course, covetousness is the exact opposite of contentment. That is why Jesus said; "...*Beware of covetousness....*" (Luke 12: 15). Covetousness is at the foundation of every evil that the world has ever known.

The tenth commandment is a warning against covetousness: "*Thou shalt not covet thy neighbour's house, thou shalt not covet thy neighbour's wife, nor his manservant, nor his maidservant, nor his ox, nor his ass, nor anything that is thy neighbour's"* Exo. 20: 17. The rule of thumb in dealing with covetousness is, anything that is not your own, take your eyes off it.

When God told the Israelites not to covet their neighbour's house, he was simply saying "be content with your own house". Of course, that does not mean you cannot desire a better house for yourself. It simply means depend on God for a better house in His timing.

I recently met a young man who told me the story of his life. He had gone through so many painful things in life in his quest to attain financial freedom. He had no formal education because his father, who is polygamous, did not pay attention to his mother and her children. This young man then began the struggle for survival right from childhood but could not really hit his target until he gave his life to Christ. He is still far from where he is going, but in his struggle he made a statement that blessed me. He said, "In my struggle for greatness, I don't want it by all means, I want it by God's means". This kind of statement is a good attack on the spirit of covetousness.

When God said, "thou shalt not covet thy neighbour's wife", He was saying, "be content with your own wife". This is corroborated in Proverbs 5: 18-20: *"Let thy fountain be blessed: and rejoice with the wife of thy youth. Let her be as the loving hind and pleasant roe; let her breasts satisfy thee at all times; and be thou ravished always with her love. And why wilt thou, my son, be ravished with a strange woman, and embrace the bosom of a stranger?"*

This is a sexual boundary that God has set for His people. As far as God is concerned, the confine of marriage is the only license for sex. It is unfortunate however, that today, many have stepped out of God's boundary for sex. Many are not contented with their wives or husbands as the case may be.

It is common place to find a married man engaged with another woman that is not his own in a sexual relationship. The converse is also true, where you find a married woman that is in a conjugal relationship with another man. The solution to the lewdness that our society finds itself today lies in a man being content with his wife and a woman being content with her husband. Of course, it also lies in a young man and a young lady waiting to be married before expressing themselves sexually.

"Marriage should be honoured by all, and the marriage bed kept pure, for God will judge the adulterer and all the sexually immoral" Heb. 13: 4 NIV.

For the married, God wants you to be content with your wife. It is understood that sometimes, your spouse may not be the ideal person you want. That should not jeopardize your marriage in any way. The truth is, there is no ideal person on earth, there are only real people. If your spouse is a difficult person in any area you see it, remember that everybody responds to love. All you need to do is to show enough love and the response will amaze you.

Lack of contentment in marriage is a possible reason for divorce. Surprisingly, the rate of divorce in our society is on the increase as statistics reveal. Whatever reason or reasons the society advances for this ugly trend is not acceptable to God. The boundary that God has set for man in this area is one man, one woman in a permanent marital relationship until death separates them.

"I hate divorce says the LORD GOD of Israel..." Mal. 2: 16 NIV.

There is no justifiable explanation for what God says He hates. The fact that a bishop is involved in a divorce does not make God to hate it any less.

I was in a Christian workers' meeting sometimes ago and we were dealing with the issue of divorce and re-marriage, an issue which has eaten deep into the Church of our time. In that meeting, a Christian brother stood up and told us a story. He said, there was a pastor that he knew personally back in his home town that had his wife divorced him. The understanding of the pastor was that he should remain unmarried. But that after sometimes, his Church members felt for him so much that they gave him permission to go and re-marry. When I heard that story, a question sprang up in my mind, "who are Church members to give permission for what God has forbidden?" It is sacrilegious for Church members to permit their pastor to enter into error.

God's Advice

Keep your lives free from the love of money and be content with what you have, because God has said, "Never will I leave you; never will I forsake you" Heb. 13: 5 NIV.

The love of money is said to be the root of all evil. God's holy book, the Bible provides a way out of the root of all evil. First, it says "keep your lives free from the love of money". One way to know that you love money is your insatiable desire to accumulate wealth. In as much as there is nothing wrong with wealth, there is everything wrong with a strong affection for wealth accumulation. Each time you find it difficult to give for the cause of the kingdom, watch out, the love of money is gaining ground in your life.

A story was told of a man who was a faithful tithe payer and was struggling to survive. This man approached his pastor for prayers so that God will intervene in his life. Not long after the pastor prayed for him, he lost his job. Then he felt so bad and went back to his pastor to ask him this question, 'why should I loose my job after prayers?' The pastor explained and encouraged him not to worry. The truth is that, sometimes God allows the worst to happen before He gives you the best. After two weeks, God gave that man a job that was approximately twelve times better in salary than the first one. He was so excited about that.

After about six months on his new job, this man had a serious trouble which took him back to his pastor. What was the trouble? He was struggling to pay his tithe. He felt that the tithe he was paying was too much for him to give to God, so he went to get some counsel from the pastor. The pastor sympathized with him concerning the struggle he was going through to pay his tithe when he had a better job, compared to the past when it was easier for him to pay his tithe. The pastor's advice was; "why don't we agree in prayer that God should reduce your salary to such a level that you could conveniently pay your tithe?" Obviously, the man screamed a big 'NO' to the pastor's suggestion.

The problem with this man was that when he began to earn so much money, he fell in love with the money and will not love to part with it. There is a way a man could love money so much that he becomes possessed of it. A rich man once approached Jesus and told Him his life's testimony. He told Jesus how he had kept the Ten Commandments from his youth to adulthood. His testimony could have placed him in the Guinness book of records of his time. I am not sure anyone had such a testimony before him. Of course, Jesus could not dispute his record. All that Jesus did was to instruct him to go sell all he had, distribute to the poor and come follow Jesus. The Bible has it on record that the man left sorrowful (Matt. 19: 16-22).

The man, who went to Jesus boasting, left sorrowful. Why? The love of money had possessed him. History

17

is replete with people who committed suicide because they lost their fortunes.

The Bible's way of dealing with the spirit of mammon is, "*keep your lives free from the love of money...*" Heb. 13: 5 NIV.

I hear somebody say how? The answer is, "*set your affection on things above, not on things on the earth*" Col. 3: 2. Heaven consciousness puts money in its proper place.

The second provision in God's word says, "*...Be content with what you have....*" Heb. 13: 5 NIV.

To watch out for discontentment in your life, check out how grateful you are to God. A believer who has found contentment in God will be grateful always. It was Ron Kenoly who sang "In your presence, I am content". God's presence ought to be enough for you if you are not too greedy as a believer.

The concluding part of Heb. 13: 5 NIV says, "*Never will I leave you; never will I forsake you*". In all of the earth, there is no greater wealth than the presence of God.

"*...In thy presence there is fullness of joy; at thy right hand there are pleasures for ever more*" Ps. 16:11. My submission is this: if you have God's presence you have everything.

Within every man lies a God-shaped vacuum which only God can fill. No material possession, no wealth, no achievement of any kind can fill this vacuum in man.

The Solution

The solution to the cravings of man is not in having more, it is in knowing that God is enough for us. The knowledge that God is enough for us brings contentment and gives the wisdom to apply one's heart to the cautionary statement of Proverbs 5: 15; *"Drink waters out of thine own cistern, and running waters out of thine own well"*.

God has made provision for His own people and we are expected to stay within the boundary of His provision for us. That is what contentment is all about. Often times, happiness is elusive except we learn to be content with what the Almighty has made available for us.

Chapter Three

What About Self-Control?

"But the fruit of the Spirit is love, joy, peace, patience, kindness, goodness, faithfulness, gentleness and self control. Against such things there is no law" Gal. 5: 22-23 (NIV).

SELF-CONTROL IS A GOOD PART OF our spirituality. You are not completely spiritual if you lack self control. When a man lacks self-control, he steps out of God's boundary at all times.

Somebody once said, out of the nine components of the fruit of the Spirit, God seems to have reserved the most difficult for the last. I beg to disagree with the statement, because self-control, like any other component of the fruit of the Spirit ought to be automatic as we respond to the Spirit.

If someone was hired to write the autobiography of Samson, his life could well be captured as "the anointed man who lacked self-control". Samson was so anointed that any nation that dares lock him in could have a security challenge. He will go for the gate and that nation will become defenseless by the following morning. Such was the anointing which he carried. Unfortunately, such an anointed man could not close his eyes to a harlot (Judges 16). What a contradiction!

The Bible says, he who is able to rule his spirit is better than he that takes a city (Prov. 16: 32).

While Samson could take a city, he could not rule over his spirit. The strength of a man of God does not lie in his anointing; it lies in his ability to remain conquered for Christ.

Anger, a Step Out of Control

I grew up as a quiet bad boy much of my life until I became born again at age eighteen. Although I did not stay committed to my profession as a Christian until about two years later when I did it again. Part of my bad nature at the time was my quick temper. I used to be very angry at the slightest provocation. I have had instances where I used sharp objects to cut people to the point of bleeding because of anger. I have had times that I poured hot liquids on my younger brother in our growing up days, for quite some simple reasons. On one occasion, I had used a table tennis bat to cause injury on the head of a young boy while playing table tennis; all because I was losing the game and the boy provoked me. The list could go on and on. The summary of it was that anger took hold of a good part of me in those days. The testimony I have today is that almost automatically, when I gave my life to Christ, the anger disappeared. I can't explain it. Today, one of the most difficult things you can do to me is to get me angry. That is certainly the power of the new birth in Christ Jesus.

When a man gets angry, he loses control of his emotions. Unexpectedly, today's world is full of angry people, some of which are Church members. When a man becomes angry, he does the unexpected. This statement reminds me of a pastor whom I know personally in Benin City, Edo state of Nigeria. This man of God was preaching on a Sunday morning in a small Church, of which I was part of the congregation that day. All of a sudden, a group of people arrived at the Church premises and ordered everybody out of the Church. Their reason was that the pastor did not own the property on which the Church was located. As at the time of their arrival, the pastor was actually concluding the Sunday school teaching. Their coming infuriated the pastor so much that he left the pulpit, pulled off his suit and was up in arms with the leader of the group. At the end of the whole episode, the pastor brought so much disgrace to the Church because of his display of anger. An angry man could be so out of control that he becomes not only a disappointment to himself, but to others also.

Have you ever thought of how foolish you acted when you were angry? Anger is a negative emotion that is a bad master if it grips its subject. Sadly, when anger is in place, it drives you out of the boundary of peace, kindness and gentleness which God has set for believers. Often times, the devil hides behind anger to wreck havoc. I can say assuredly, without fear of contradiction, that an angry man could be an instrument of cruelty in the hands of the devil.

When Simeon and Levi were angry because their sister, Dinah was raped, they brought pain to the whole city. They deceived the men of the city and asked them to be circumcised as a condition to give out their sister to Shechem for marriage. The people consented and were circumcised, but while they were still nursing the pain of circumcision, Simeon and Levi came upon them in anger and slew them (Gen. 34: 25-29). Their anger and the consequence of it pained the heart of their father up to the point of his death. Hear what their father had to say concerning their anger at the point of his death:

"*Simeon and Levi are brethren; instrument of cruelty are in their habitations. O my soul, come not thou into their secret; unto their assembly, mine honour, be not thou united: for in their anger they slew a man, and in their self will they digged down a wall. Cursed be their anger, for it was fierce; and their wrath, for it was cruel: I will divide them in Jacob, and scatter them in Israel*" Gen. 49: 5-7.

Can you see what anger can do? It brings division and it causes a scattering. Anger can divide families; it can scatter lives and nations.

A Good Anger?

Well, some people call it holy anger. Is there anything called a holy anger? Okay, let's agree that the anger that makes you mad at the devil is a holy anger. The kind of anger that made Jesus mad at the people who turned His father's house to a den of robbers, could as much qualify as a holy anger (Matt. 21: 12-13). But remember, the anger of Jesus was not devastating. It is difficult to admit, but there may be an anger that does not lead to sin. The Bible says, *"Be angry, and sin not: let not the sun go down upon your wrath"* Eph. 4: 26.

Anger and sin are twin brothers. That is why the Bible says, as soon as you get angry, make sure it doesn't lead to sin. The way to go about anger which should not lead to sin is to tame it. How do you tame anger? The next time someone makes you angry, just walk away. That may be difficult, but it is wisdom. When you are so angry, make sure you don't talk and you don't act. This is because talking is one way of venting your anger, and it could be catastrophic. When your emotions overwhelm you, the wise thing to do is to put a pad lock on your lips.

The next thing to do to anger is to make sure it doesn't last. *"...Let not the sun go down on your anger"* Eph. 4: 26. The fact is; when anger is short-lived, the devil is kept at bay. Why must we not allow anger to last? This is because a long-lived anger does much harm. Should not we learn from God who can be angry at us because of our sins, but does not allow his anger to last?

"For his anger endureth but a moment...." Ps. 30: 5.

To God be the glory, whose anger lasts for just a moment, but who has loved us with an everlasting love (Jer. 31: 3).

Self-Control or Discipline?

The hall mark of discipleship is the ability to deny one's self in order to be able to follow the Master.

Jesus told His disciples, *"...If any man will come after me, let him deny himself and take up his cross and follow me"* Matt. 16: 24.

Discipleship is actually a call to self denial. According to Abraham Joshua Heschel: "Self-respect is the root of discipline: The sense of dignity grows with the ability to say no to one's self". The ability to say no to one's self, which is self-control, seems to be more difficult than climbing Mount Carmel.

Why is it that some people fall into avoidable sin? It is largely due to lack of self-control. You could see a believer who is caught in a web of adultery or fornication and will refuse to take responsibility for it, but simply blame it on the devil. It is not much of the devil for a man to fall into sin, as it is much of his flesh which is left uncontrolled.

When Paul the apostle was struggling with sin in his life (Romans 7: 15-25), he identified the culprit. Clearly, the culprit was his flesh. He called it "sin that dwelleth in me" vs. 17. He called this same nature "another law in my members" vs23. The flesh in man is like the law of gravity that pulls a man down when he wants to go up. For Paul the apostle, this law made him wretched until he encountered the power of Christ.

The flesh is a corrosive agent in the human soul which must be inhibited in order to go far in life. Any man who takes his flesh for granted is going down hill. In most cases, the flesh or the untamed nature in man is the undoing of many people. Brother Gbile Akani once said, "Sin is the pampering of the flesh". The disciples of Jesus were found wanting at the hour that Jesus needed them most. Jesus was in so much agony when the time of his death on the cross drew near. He took some of His disciples with Him to the place of prayer and requested that they should watch with Him. But to His amazement, in less than an hour, the disciples had all slept. Even in His pain and disappointment, Jesus was able to identify the problem with His disciples. He told them plainly, "the spirit indeed is willing, but the flesh is weak" (Matt. 26: 36-46).

It is not a new discovery that the flesh is strong in physical things, but weak in spiritual things. No wonder why you see people who could sit for hours to watch movies, find it difficult to pray for 30 minutes without sleeping off. It is the weakness of the flesh in spiritual things that is responsible for this. For a man to conquer the flesh, he must learn to surrender it to the Spirit.

Only in absolute surrender to the Spirit is the flesh a subject.

Church discipline, even though old fashioned, is a measure put in place to correct those who lack self-control. While self-control is an internal mechanism put in place to checkmate the excesses of the flesh, discipline is an external provision to correct a misbehaviour that was not curtailed by self-control. Self-control is the break that you apply when the flesh wants to speed off track.

In some advanced countries, there are speed limits for motorists. It takes self-control for motorists who enjoy speed to maintain this limit. To check a violation of this limit, the government of such nations put in place a fine. If you exceed the limit and you get caught, you are made to pay a fine. That is discipline. Why did they put disciplinary measures in place? They put it to help people apply the breaks when the limit is being exceeded. The judicial arm of government in a democracy is also there to help people apply the breaks in order not to exceed the limits that the society has set for its people.

Within every man lies a consciousness of limits that God has set and it takes self-control to stay within the limits, failure of which attracts the wrath of God. The wrath of God is a disciplinary measure that God has put in place to help mankind apply the breaks when the limit is being exceeded. It is not out of place to consider

HIV/AIDS as the wrath of God to help mankind to apply the breaks, in order not to exceed the limit that God has set for sexual expression. Unfortunately, men have invented the use of condom instead of abstinence. May God give us understanding.

What is Addiction?

Addiction is getting used to the pleasures of sin, as motivated by the flesh and left untamed by the failure of self-control. Drug addicts have a form of pleasure in drugs before they became addicted. It is my opinion that the devil cannot give you what you are not willing to take.

When the devil came to Mrs. Adam in the Garden of Eden in what can be regarded as the first temptation, he simply played on her interest. He asked the woman if God had said she should not eat of every tree in the garden. She replied the devil that God restricted them from eating from the fruit of the tree in the midst of the garden. The devil disputed what God had told her and then he worked on her psychology. By the time the devil was through, the woman was left to decide (Gen. 3: 1-7).

"And when the woman saw that the tree was good for food, and that it was pleasant to the eyes, and a tree to be desired to make one wise, she took of the fruit thereof, and did eat, and gave also unto her husband with her; and he did eat" Gen. 3: 6.

Here, the devil gave the woman an opportunity to sin and she had the desire to sin. An opportunity to sin and a desire to sin is a bad combination. In my book, "The grace of God" I wrote and said; Grace is when God takes away the desire to sin when there is an opportunity to sin, and also when He takes away the opportunity to sin when the desire to sin is there.

It could have been a different story, if when the devil came to Eve with the opportunity she had no desire for it. She would have kept the devil at bay. You will notice that it was not the devil who gave the fruit to the woman, she went for it. The problem was not in the fact that the devil came to tempt the woman, but that he made her to go for what God had forbidden. The same devil actually tempted Jesus also, but the difference was that Jesus was not interested in what the devil suggested to him. Every temptation is a suggestion from the devil; it takes interest in order to yield. Once you agree to the devil's first temptation, your defence is broken and it becomes easier to do more evil. All drug addicts, alcoholics, prostitutes and so on, simply agreed to the first temptation and then they became trapped in it.

The Trouble Called Lasciviousness

"Now the works of the flesh are manifest, which are these; Adultery, fornication, uncleanness, lasciviousness" Gal. 5: 19.

For a long time in my growing up days as a believer the word "lasciviousness was a big word to understand until I did a little study on the word. The Greek word behind the English word lascivious is aselgeia. It occurs nine times in the New Testament. Twice it is rendered wantonness. Once it appears as filthy. Six times it is translated as lascivious.

Lasciviousness is a gross form of wickedness which has sexual overtones in many cases. In a phrase it means "unbridled life". Put it differently, it means "unrestrained life". It suggests a disregard for public decency. The word lasciviousness is translated indecency in the Amplified version of the holy book, the Bible. The term "aselgeia" goes beyond sexual sin and connotes any form of excess i.e. one who knows no boundaries in whatever form of evil he indulges.

The above definitions of lasciviousness paint a big picture of the society we live in. It appears as if today's society has lost all the sense of the boundaries that exist. The looseness that we see, the indecency in dressing which is common place, the inordinate affections that are rampant, the agitation for gay rights that are evident are all pointers to this fact. There is no greater mess than that a man steps out of God's boundary.

When Adam and Eve fell, the first practical solution that God provided for them was clothing to cover their nakedness. How comes today's world delights herself in exposing her nakedness? Several celebrities around the world are known by the breasts they expose, the hot legs they display and the sexual image that they wear. Such is the moral decadence of our time!

The first marriage which God blessed was that of Adam - a man and Eve - a woman. How comes this generation wants to reverse it? Why do they want to marry man to man and woman to woman? Such is the corruption of the mind which has eaten deep into some folks. I sometimes wonder, if it is the "gross darkness" which the Bible says will cover the people? (Isaiah 60: 2). If it is, then it is high time that the Church began to shine, so that the Gentiles may come to our light. This need is much more urgent, because darkness is encroaching into the Church. Oh Lord, help the Church to arise and confront this menace by the power of the light before our light is turned into darkness!

The Way Out

The creature called man was not created to have his own way, but rather for God to have His way in him. When the songwriter, Adelaide Pollard wrote the song 'Have your own way, have your own way, you are the potter I am the clay', she was simply surrendering to God in order to live a fulfilled life. Only in absolute surrender to God does the human soul finds its highest expression. When we allow God to have His way in us, He restrains us from certain lifestyles and opens our hearts to pour His love that constrains us and keep us within the reach of His love. The finest moments of our lives is realized when we constrain ourselves within the limits of His love.

Chapter Four

Choose Humility

A STORY WAS TOLD ABOUT A brother who gave his life to Christ and became very dedicated to the service of the kingdom in his local assembly. As he was growing in the things of the Lord, one of the virtues that quickly manifested in his life was humility. This brother was so humble; you could easily mistake him for Moses, whom the Bible described as the meekest on earth. His local assembly decided one day to honour him as the most humble person in the congregation. So, they organized an award which was presented to him in the presence of the whole congregation. It was such an honour!

The following day, this brother started carrying the award about to show to people that he was the most humble person. In actual sense, he lost his humility the moment he started carrying his award about in order to show it to people.

This story tells of how difficult it is for humble people to remain so, especially at the peak of success. There are actually not many humble people in life, and the few humble ones have the tendency to lose this virtue, with the attainment of some level of success.

King Uzziah was only sixteen years old when he ascended the throne. By all standards, he was a minor in today's world. At best he would have been in college trying to study in a field of human endeavour. But God picked him up to be king in the stead of his father. It is a great lesson to learn, that God does not always follow the protocols of men in His choice of leaders. Anyway, as of the time that God picked him up, he was a godly teenager. He did that which was right in the sight of God and he sought after God in the days of Zecharia the prophet. We could rightly say this teenager was a novice in leadership role, but he was not a novice in spiritual things.

To his credit, he had understanding in the visions of God. This certainly placed him on the path of greatness. Of course, any man who understands the visions of God for his life has been set up for greatness in life. So, it is not surprising that the Lord made Uzziah to prosper in such a dimension as recorded in Scriptures. He did not only defeat the Philistines, he built cities in the enemies' territories. That is not a mean achievement at all. As if that was not enough, God helped him not only against the Philistines, but also against the Arabians. And then the Ammonites, who were 'sworn enemies' of Israel, paid tributes to him. This achievement made him to become famous as far as to Egypt. The kind of military might which he had was unprecedented in his days. If it was today, his military armament would have unsettled the super powers. His type of military intelligence would have produced the most sophisticated nuclear war head of our time. You will notice that their military adventure did not impact negatively on their economy. They were able to dig many wells, they had plenty cattle, they had agriculturalists that were cultivating the land for food production. Make no mistake about his achievements it was because God marvelously helped him (2 Chro. 26; 1-15). My submission is, "No man does this kind of thing except the Lord be with him". It sounds in tune with Nicodemous' submission when he went to Jesus by night (John 3: 1-2). Please understand that there are no great acts outside the great God.

On a very sad note however, Uzziah allowed pride in his life and it ruined all his achievements. Bible record has it that: "...*when he was strong, his heart was lifted up to his destruction*...." 2 Chro. 26:16.

The ugly part of his history came at the entrant of pride. It is difficult to say whether it is right to pray against pride, or to simply watch against pride at the peak of success. Lord, have mercy! In the words of a man of God, "Pride is the siren that alerts people that you are about to fall". This is exactly what the Bible meant when it says, *"Pride goes before destruction, a haughty spirit before a fall"* (Prov. 16: 18 NIV).

Being Sorry

One of the manifestations of humility is in the ability to say sorry, when the need arises. A husband and wife had lived together joyfully for years. Theirs was a blissful home which was the envy of neighbours around. One day, they had a major misunderstanding that shook the foundation of the home. The wife demanded an apology from her husband as a solution to the crisis. The ego in the man will not allow him to say sorry, in order to settle the matter. In my opinion, saying sorry is a simple solution to complex conflicts.

As simple as saying sorry is, it is an up hill task for the proud. Most relationships are destroyed at the onset of pride. Somehow, people don't get to realize that pride is a destroyer of relationships. You will notice that for most strained relationships, the golden words, "I am sorry" bring restoration. If two proud people get married as husband and wife, in all optimism, the end of such a marriage is predictable. Did I hear you say divorce? You cannot be more correct. Maybe one reason why we have several cases of divorce is because proud people have infiltrated into the holy estate of marriage.

Fighting and wars will end if the world will cherish being sorry. Even the anger of God is turned away, when people learn to tell Him sorry. The people of

Nineveh had committed enough sin to qualify for God's judgment. In response to the pile up of their sins, God sent Prophet Jonah to warn them that in forty days the city will be destroyed. When they heard the message from God, all of them in unison repented of their sins, in fasting and in ashes (Jonah 3). That was their way of saying sorry to God. Jehovah's response to their being sorry was an aversion of the promised judgment. Nothing turns away the anger of God like being sorry. The difference between the city of Nineveh and the land of Sodom was that, while Nineveh had opportunity to say sorry for their sins, Sodom had no room for repentance.

Perhaps, one of the greatest secrets which David knew about God, was Jehovah's inability to turn away from a people that are sorry. That knowledge made David to be quick to repentance each time he sinned. Of course, with this attitude, he earned the prestigious title of 'the man after God's heart'. Oh! That man will learn to say sorry to God and fellow man when the need arises.

Condescending

The greatest lesson of humility which Jesus showed to humanity was that he left the glory of Heaven and came to the earth which He created. The reality of humility can be seen in condescension. When the Bible demanded that we should condescend to men of low estate (Rom. 12: 16), it was simply appealing to the nature of Christ in us. Of course, this nature in us needs our cooperation for it to manifest itself. Phil. 2: 5 says, *"Let this mind be in you, which was also in Christ Jesus"*. The full expression of the mind of Christ in terms of humility is realized only in collaboration with our consent. Thanks to God who has not left us without an example of humility, as we see in the Lord Jesus.

Obviously, Jesus was a man of reputation, but He deliberately made Himself of no reputation. How many people of reputation can make themselves of no reputation and condescend to men of low estate? I am afraid, if Jesus was physically on earth today, and he needed to fly in an aircraft, He may not have to fly in First class. You will notice that most of His associations while on earth were with commoners. Is there a lesson or two for us to learn from His lifestyle? Yes, there are many! First, if Jesus was a professor, He will not feel too lofty to be relevant to the uneducated. Second, if He was a medical doctor, He will not walk down the road as having the most prestigious job. Third, if He was a pilot, He will not berate others. Fourth, if He was an army general, He will not be carried away by the euphoria of military statesmanship. What more shall I say? Don't let your reputation stand between you and good relationship with all classes of men. In that way, you are condescending to men of low estate, and by the way, that is practical humility!

Doing Menial Jobs

He trained as an accountant in a famous University in Nigeria. After his graduation, he wanted to practice in his field of study. He walked through the city of Lagos, Nigeria in search of an accounting job. All his efforts met a brick wall. At a point, he became discouraged and was not willing to try any more, his uncle suggested that he should try something different. The uncle suggested that he should join a group of people to off load yams which come in trucks from different villages to the city of Lagos, Nigeria. Reluctantly, he began doing the suggested business. Some months later, he graduated from off loading of yams. He started going to the villages to get yams to the city. Not long, he became an employer of labour. He actually became a business consultant who sits in his luxurious office and people come to consult him. That was the startling story of a young man who became wealthy by starting with a menial job. The courage of this young man should be saluted, because it takes humility for an accountant to do the dirty job of bringing down yams from trucks.

Humility can be expressed in our willingness to do menial jobs. Some anointed brothers cannot be asked to mob toilets. They are 'too anointed' to do such a dirty job. The question is, 'how does a man get promoted, if not in the place of humility?' When Jesus humbled Himself and became obedient, even to the point of death, God in response to His humility highly exalted Him and gave Him an irresistible name.

Humility in the sight of God is like a precious ointment that gives Him a lee way to bless a man. Pride on the other hand, is what gives God a justification to resist a man. Assuredly, the man that God resists cannot go far in life.

Remember, God is watching you when in humility you do the so-called menial assignments that are assigned to you. This statement reminds me of an incidence that happened to me recently. At our local level, the Pentecostal Fellowship of Nigeria (PFN) held an election of executives into various offices. The election started from the highest local office of a coordinator down to the office of a treasurer. Incidentally, I went to that meeting at the instance of my pastor as an observer. I watched all the 'lucrative' offices shared and at the end of it all, I was made the treasurer. I felt berated as a pastor to be elected as a keeper of money. I made a move to reject it, but the demand by the people was compelling. Finally, I accepted it knowing fully well that there is no assignment that is too menial for the humble.

Showing Respect

Respect is said to be reciprocal and must be reciprocated. Can this sage hold water among the proud? It is doubtful. It is easier for a proud man to expect respect, than he is willing to give it. A respectful man is courteous and he gives consideration to others above self. The golden rule says, "Do to others what you will have them do to you". This rule could very well define what true respect is all about. In all relationships, when the parties involved observe the rule of respect, such relationships blossom to the admiration of the world. One of the wives of David, Michal, who happened to be the daughter of Saul, had an occasion to disrespect her husband. The husband had just returned with the ark of the Lord back to Israel, with such pomp and excitement! He danced so much that his nakedness was exposed unknown to him. Michal, who looked through the window to catch a glimpse of the king, was surprised at what she saw. When the king returned home, rather than giving him a rousing welcome, she spoke to him with such a disdain. The husband in his response gave her a disgusting answer. It was like paying evil for evil (2 Sam. 6: 20-23). In my analysis of that episode, I guess it may not be the first time that they had such a show of disrespect. Whatever it is, it is inglorious to be in a relationship without mutual respect for each other.

Learning to Accept Mistakes

There are people who make mistakes and refuse to accept it. What kind of spirit is that? It is the spirit of pride. It is a sign of pride when one tries to explain an obvious mistake. It is not right to explain a mistake, it is only proper to accept, correct and learn from it. Somehow, when people are not willing to accept their mistakes, they end up making more mistakes. Why will a young unmarried lady who becomes pregnant by mistake, opt for abortion? The straight answer is that she is not willing to accept her mistake. So, her mistake costs her the life of an innocent baby.

The first mistake David made which painted a part of his history black was that at the time when kings went to war, he sat back at home. This is like being in the wrong place at the wrong time. Next, he decided to climb the roof top to have an areal view of his country. Rather than seeing the beauty of his country, the devil directed his eyes to the beauty of a naked woman. For sure, not many men can close their eyes to the nakedness of a woman. He immediately sent for the woman. It is not likely that the woman went to the palace naked. The fact that she dressed herself before going to the palace would have been enough to cool down David's sexual drive towards her. But the king did not let go the picture he saw. This led to the sin of adultery which resulted in pregnancy. Everything happened too fast! Rather than accept his mistake, David was better prepared to cover it. David had a plan. He called back Uriah from the battle field at the jeopardy of the whole army of Israel. When Uriah will not accept David's deceptive plan to go home and sleep with his wife, at the expense of losing the battle, the king rolled out a plan B; that plan B was suicidal. It ended the life of a General in the army of Israel; all in David's bid to cover his mistake (2 Sam. 11: 5-27). Refusing to accept mistakes can be so devastating!

Let's take for granted that an average human being has a bad nature. That nature is better stimulated when pride is factored in. That was what compounded David's problem. For sure, David received his due punishment from God. The lesson is; man was not designed to escape God's judgment when he commits sin, except through repentance, confession and obtaining of forgiveness by His mercy. Even then, there could still be a repercussion. The truth is, when a man is too proud to confess his sins, he has built an apartment for himself in hell.

Willingness to Learn

The cost of ignorance is said to be more than the price we pay for knowledge. Be that as it may, it is even more expensive to be unwilling to learn. Life actually has many lessons to learn from. But the proud man will rather choose his folly of watching rather than learn from life. There are people who don't know some things, but out of pride refuse to ask questions. One of the indicators of pride is in not willing to ask questions when in need of answers.

One of the secrets of doing well in life is learning, and part of the learning process includes asking questions. The prophet Isaiah, who is unarguably one of the most powerful prophets that ever lived, made a very simple statement in Isaiah 1: 17 *"learn to do well..."* The statement above is indicative of the fact that doing well in life is a function of learning. How much a man is willing to learn predisposes him towards excellence in life.

Submission

Being submissive is one way we display humility. When God in His wisdom requested that the woman should submit to her husband, even though it looks like a difficult task to the woman, it is God's way of testing her humility. In a group, when the individuals involved clothe themselves with a submissive spirit, it engenders the spirit of team work. And wherever there is a team work, success becomes a lot easier to achieve. Take a very successful foot ball team for example, to a great extent their team spirit determines their winning stride. If everybody in the team decides to play for himself as an individual, the chances are very high that they will loose the match. But a football match becomes very entertaining when the players play as a team. If organizations are able to borrow lessons from a foot ball game, they are bound to meet organizational goals more easily.

When Mary the mother of Jesus had an angelic visitation, the discourse that ensued between her and the angel was revealing. The angel had delivered to her the message from the Lord and she became a bit worried. Her worry was understandable because she was a virgin and could not imagine how she would give birth to the Saviour of the world. The angel took time to explain to her how the miracle would happen. Then Mary submitted herself to the Lord (Luke 1: 26-38). This you could see in her statement; "...*Behold the handmaid of the Lord; be it unto me according to thy word....*"

Luke. 1: 38. It was her submission that sealed the miraculous conception of the Saviour of the world. We must learn to submit ourselves both to God, and to authorities. For in so doing, we plant the seed of blessing in our destinies.

Decrease for God's Increase

It was John the Baptist who made the remark that he will decrease for Christ to increase (John 3: 30). The import of his expression is that, as believers we must learn to minimize our image and maximize the image of Christ in us. When we deliberately refuse to project ourselves and insist on promoting the Christ nature in us, we are decreasing while Christ is increasing. It is in this practice that our lives become attractive in bringing people to Christ. Jesus said, *"And I, If I be lifted up from the earth, will draw all men unto me"* (Jn. 12: 32). Jesus cannot be lifted up in a vacuum; He can only be lifted up in our lives. Let our lives point men to Christ, let our testimonies be Christ-centered and let everything 'us' be all about Him. In so doing, we make Christ to flow through us to the outside world.

The greatest message of salvation can be relayed by the lifestyle of the believer. Jesus is undoubtedly the answer to the world today, but the world finds it difficult to accept it because we have not been effective in communicating it. When the Bible says, we are the written epistle of Christ (2 Cor. 3: 2-3), it is a wake up call to be careful how we live. The believer is a type of communication port, our lifestyle is the message that we send to the world about Christ. When we humble ourselves, and allow Christ to live His life in us, our assignment of communicating Christ becomes easy.

The Lesson

Looking at all that have been discussed about humility in this chapter, it is like a mineral prospector stumbling into a gold mine! The beauty of humility sparkles; it directs us away from self and points us towards God. Humility keeps us in check and once we are in check, we remain within God's boundary.

Chapter Five

Loving God

THE FOUR LETTERED WORD 'LOVE' IS perhaps the most popular word today. An average adult must have used that word for several dozen times. Love forms the motif of most movies. It is scintillating to listen to love stories. Somehow, the world is in an 'elusive' search for love. In an elusive search because it lacks the correct definition of love. Wherever there is a proper definition of terms or concepts, a major hurdle is crossed. Love is not the emotional attachment between a man and a woman. It is not the sweet sensation that two people feel for each other. It is rather a deep connection which transcends emotion.

Unlike faith, which the Bible defines as the substance of things hoped for, the evidence of things not seen (Heb. 11: 1), love has no biblical definition. It only has biblical demonstration!

"For God so loved the world, that he gave his only begotten Son, that whosoever believeth in him should not perish, but have everlasting life" Jn. 3: 16.

When God did a spiritual calculation, He came to the conclusion that man cannot understand the definition of love; he can only be captivated by its demonstration. The greatest story of love ever told, is that of the Saviour dying for sinners. Perhaps one of the greatest weaknesses that the devil has is he cannot withstand the story of love being told to sinners. That is why he will stop at nothing to hinder the gospel from spreading. But God's love cannot be stopped.

When the Bible says, "For God so loved the world", it is talking about an intensive love. When a patient in the hospital is moved to an intensive care unit, it means he is to be given special attention owing to the critical nature of his condition. At such times, the doctors and nurses give in their best to rescue the patient. Similarly, when God was on a rescue mission, He gave us His best to save us from our critical conditions of sin. There is no greater love than this, that a man laid down his life for his friends (Jn. 15: 13).

What Manner of Love!

Sometimes ago, I read a magazine, "The Ever Increasing Kingdom" written by my son in the faith, Seye Davids. In that magazine, he narrates this story of love: In a kingdom where slavery was legal, a certain nobleman met a slave bidding process in a crowded street. He paused to observe the activities and as he watched from the edge of the crowd, he saw one slave after another led unto a platform with their arms and legs shackled with ropes like animals. Standing before the jeering crowd, they were auctioned, one after another.

While the nobleman studied the group of slaves waiting nearby, he saw a young girl standing at the back. Her eyes were filled with fear; she looked so frightened. Shortly, it was her turn to be auctioned. The nobleman offered twice the amount ever offered for any slave at that fair in order to have the slave girl. With silence from the audience, the gavel fell and the young girl was sold to the nobleman. Not happy with her new owner, the young girl looked into his face and spat on him. With smile on his face, he reached out for a handkerchief and wiped his face of the spittle. The deal was concluded with the papers signed and handed over to the nobleman. Rather than keep the document, he handed it over to the slave girl and told her, "I bought you to set you free".

The nobleman's statement was unbelievable. But the slave girl soon came to the realization of his statement. She fell to her knees and wept at his feet. With tears of joy and gratitude, she asked, "You bought me to set me free?" Then she proclaimed: "I'll serve you forever!" She followed him without a chain but bound willingly by a cord of gratitude. She didn't claim any rights with him, only an obligation of love and duty! What manner of love is this? This kind of love cannot be explained, it can only be responded to. And the most appropriate response is to willingly become a captive of love.

Incidentally, the above story is a familiar one. Jesus paid with His blood the price to set us free from the slavery of sin.

Paul the apostle reported what Jesus did as a demonstration of love, when he said: *"You were bought with a price (purchased with a preciousness and paid for, made His own). So then, honor God and bring glory to Him in your body."* (1 Cor. 6: 20 AMP).

It is wonderful to know that our bride price wasn't some piece of cowries, but the precious blood of the only Son of God! That tells a lot about our worth in the sight of God. You may not think you are worth anything much, but in God's sight you are a precious jewel.

When John the beloved was to summarize the love story of God to mankind, he did it in a captivating way: *"HOW GREAT is the love the Father has lavished on us, that we should be called children of God! And that is what we are!..."* 1 John 3: 1 NIV.

This great love of God should place a demand on our lives. It should be a demand of a loving relationship with Him. There is nothing we need on this side of eternity that God has not already given by the love He demonstrated. A slave of love will ask for nothing from the master, but remains eternally grateful for the love offering.

The Starting Point

At the start of this chapter, I made mention of the fact that the world is in an elusive search for love. This is so because true love begins with a response to God's love. Just like the moon has no light of its own, but reflects the light of the sun, so the world has no love outside of the reflection of God's love. It means therefore, that the people who talk about love outside God are under a delusion. The eternal word of God confirms this when it says, *"Beloved, let us love one another, for love is from God; and everyone who loves is born of God and knows God. The one who does not love does not know God, for God is love"* 1 Jn. 4: 7-8 NAS.

As a baby is connected to the mother via the umbilical cord in the womb, so is love connected to God. You really cannot disconnect love from God. In order to experience real love you must accept God's love.

There seems to be a good connection between love and the knowledge of God. When somebody comes to tell you how much he loves you, find out if he knows God. If he doesn't know God, his so-called love is an invitation for trouble. There is no man outside God who can truly love. The best he can do is to sacrifice. And there is a whole lot of difference between love and sacrifice. You can sacrifice without love, but you cannot love without sacrifice. Do you not know, have you not heard that the everlasting Father, the Maker of the Heavens and the earth, showers love on His children and expects them to reciprocate same to others? No man can give love until he first receives it. The world is devoid of love until she agrees to receive the love which God first gave to her.

Love Relationship

Every genuine relationship begins with love. The covenant relationship between David and Jonathan came as a result of love. These two people were so intimate to the extent that they made several sacrifices for each other. Theirs was a beautiful relationship. The secret was that they loved each other.

"And it came to pass, when he had made an end of speaking unto Saul, that the soul of Jonathan was knit with the soul of David, and Jonathan loved him as his own soul" 1 Sam. 18: 1.

The love of God for mankind opened an opportunity for relationship. When man accepts the love of God by receiving Jesus into his life, a whole new relationship begins. That relationship is sustained by the love which we develop towards Him who first loved us. To the extent we love Him to that extent our relationship is deepened.

It is my considered opinion that one of the reasons why some believers backslide, is because of a lack of a growing love for the Master. If our first love for Him at salvation is sustained and nurtured, it will be difficult to retrace our steps from following Him.

One thing Jesus had against the Church in Ephesus was that they had abandoned their first love.

"Nevertheless I have somewhat against thee, because thou hast left thy first love" Rev. 2: 4.

The easiest way to have a strained relationship with God is for a believer to abandon his first love. For as long as a believer's dying love for God is not checked, a step out of God's boundary is imminent.

Love for the Brethren

It is not possible to love God and not love the brethren. As a matter of fact, it's mockery of the faith to confess that we love God and yet hate a fellow believer. John the beloved tried to debunk the claim that a man can love God without loving a fellow believer when he said, *"If anyone says, "I love God", yet hates his brother, he is a liar. For anyone who does not love his brother, whom he has seen, cannot love God, whom he has not seen. And he has given us this command: Whoever loves God must also love his brother"* 1 Jn. 4: 20-21 NIV.

The law of biblical love states that when a man claims he loves God, the chances are that such a man will love his brother unconditionally. Among other things, this is what 1 Jn.4:20-21 is saying: the visible realm is the sphere of manifestation of our love to the invisible God. Put differently, there is no man that can truly reach out to God in love, while by-passing his brother who is in need of love.

There is what the Bible calls 'bowels of mercies'. This is the main outlet through which love flows to others. The word 'compassion' is actually a poor rendition for the phrase 'bowels of mercies'. But let's agree that compassion is good enough to make the point. When Jesus came to the earth, as a proof of His love, the mechanism of His wonderful acts came into play each time He was 'moved with compassion'. The first requirement in order for us to show love is for us to be clothed with a compassionate heart. Whether it is love for the brethren or for others, a compassionate heart is the pivot on which love revolves. The world would definitely have been a better place, if it was filled with people with a compassionate heart.

A look at the story of the good Samaritan which Jesus gave, points to the fact that the only reason why the good Samaritan showed kindness, was because he was moved with compassion towards the 'certain man' who fell among thieves. The priest was the first person who passed by without rendering any assistance. The next person who passed by without giving a helping hand was a Levite. Both of them did nothing about the man because they were devoid of compassion. Each time you come across people who are in trouble and you feel nothing, it is an indication of a lack of compassion. Thank God that by divine providence, a man who had a heart of compassion came around and showed that 'certain man' much kindness (Luke. 10: 30-36).

As a show of our love for people, our compassionate heart must be followed with acts of kindness. 'Bowels of mercies' and kind-heartedness are the two attributes that the believer needs in order to seal his love contract for the brethren. The wisdom therefore is, let's ask God to give us a heart of compassion and enable us to show acts of kindness.

Love for Sinners

The sin of man did not prevent God's love when Jesus was sent to die for mankind. In God's vocabulary, love is a choice word. Even the worst of sins cannot shield God's love. That is why if we truly love God, we will love sinners while hating their sins. The greatest manifestation of our love to sinners is to warn them from the dangers of hell. Next, is to do the best we can, while keeping our holy estate, to connect with their humanity. Even if we know sinners that have declared themselves as our enemies, it is erroneous to treat them so.

"Ye have heard that it hath been said, Thou shalt love thy neighbour, and hate thine enemy. But I say unto you, love your enemies, bless them that curse you, do good to them that hate you, and pray for them which despitefully use you, and persecute you; That ye may be the children of your Father which is in heaven: for he maketh his sun to rise on the evil and on the good, and sendeth rain on the just and on the unjust" Matt. 5: 43-45.

What a testament! It is an acknowledged fact that it will not be easy to love a 'known enemy'. Somehow, God is not asking us to do the impossible. It may be difficult, but it is not impossible. It makes sense to know that, the love of God was shed abroad in our hearts, so that it might spread abroad from our hearts unto others - enemies inclusive!

Does it amaze you to hear that the Heavenly Father makes His sun to rise upon both the evil and the good? It is not surprising for such to come from the benevolent God! It is not even news to hear that God does not discriminate between the farm which belongs to a sinner and that of a believer, when sending His rain. What looks strange is that God is asking believers to take a cue from Him. Wow! Believers need all the grace as far as this expectation is concerned.

Chapter Six

The Fear of God

FOR WELL OVER A DOZEN TIMES, the book of the Bible which is reputed as a fountain of wisdom; the book of Proverbs makes mention of the issue of the fear of the Lord. This is to emphasize the importance of the subject matter.

The fear of the Lord is central to the Christian faith and it must be practically applied in order for us to stay within God's confines.

Proverbs 9: 10 says, *"The fear of the LORD is the beginning of wisdom: and the knowledge of the holy is understanding"*.

The relationship between the fear of the Lord and holiness is a direct proportionality. The connection is, with the fear of God, holiness becomes practicable.

Departing from Iniquity

"By mercy and truth iniquity is purged: and by the fear of the LORD men depart from evil" Prov. 16: 6

By God's arrangement iniquity is to be departed from; and the fear of God is the motivation for such a departure. When Joseph was enticed by Portipher's wife to commit adultery with her, he refused. The motivation for such a refusal was the fear of God. This can be noticed in his statement: *"There is none greater in this house than I; neither hath he kept back anything from me but thee, because thou art his wife: how then can I do this great wickedness, and sin against God?"* Gen. 39: 9.

The language of the man who fears God is, "how can I do this great wickedness and sin against God?" Joseph did not consider the fact that the sin in question could have been covered successfully, but was aware of the fact that no man can hide his sins from God. You may cover your sins for no man else to know, but not from the Father of lights.

When Joseph refused to consent to Mrs. Portipher's demand, she did not give up on him. She continued with her evil desire until one day she had an opportunity to rape him: *"And she caught him by his garment, saying, Lie with me: and he left his garment in her hand, and fled, and got him out"* Gen. 39: 12.

When Joseph was boxed into a corner by his master's wife, the next resistance he could put up was, "he fled and got him out". He simply ran out of the house without his garment in order to preserve his relationship with God. His determination for righteousness was at a cost - his garment! Any Bible scholar could be impressed at Joseph's determination not to sin against God and his master. How much of resistance you are able to muster against temptation is determined by the level of your fear of God.

Perfecting Holiness

God's demand is that we should be holy as He is holy. Without holiness, the Bible says no man shall see the Lord (Heb 12: 14). Holiness is a pre-requisite to fulfilling our greatest aspiration as believers, which is, seeing the Lord.

When you go through the Scriptures from Genesis to Revelation, you will see clearly that God demands, propels and inspires His people towards holiness. Even the promises of God's blessings are a motivation to keep us in His Holiness. The seed of God in us at salvation is God's investment for us to be partakers of His holiness.

"Whosoever is born of God doth not commit sin; for his seed remaineth in him: and he cannot sin, because he is born of God" 1 Jn. 3: 9.

The Amplified version renders this verse more clearly: *"No one born (begotten) of God (deliberately, knowingly, and habitually) practices sin, for God's nature abides in him (His principle of life, the divine sperm, remains permanently within him); and he cannot practice sinning because he is born (begotten) of God"* 1 Jn. 3: 9 Amplified.

What more shall be said about the above verse of Scripture that has not been fully captured in the Amplified rendition? The truth is God is not requiring the fruit of holiness where He has not first sown the seed for it.

Having said all that, it is time to say that the seed of holiness sown in us when we got born again is nurtured by the fear of the Lord. That is the reason why we are admonished to perfect holiness in the fear of God. The Scripture says, *"Having therefore these promises, dearly beloved, let us cleanse ourselves from all filthiness of the flesh and spirit, perfecting holiness in the fear of God"* 2 Cor. 7: 1.

Holiness becomes more obvious as it is being perfected and its perfection is a function of the fear of the Lord in the believer's heart. The fear of God is not an emotion; it is a perception of who God is, what His demands are and the choice to stay with His demands.

The Absence of Multitude

When you are in a closet, where no one sees you, don't forget the omnipresent personality. The story was told of a man who was to commit a crime and he took caution in order not to be caught by looking left, right, backward and forward before going ahead with the act. Then his conscience pricked him, "there is one more direction you have not considered. You have not looked up to see if God is watching or not". People don't seem to fear God as much as they fear the camera. There are things that people will not do when the cameras are on, but which they will do easily off camera. The camera has power, it will catch you committing the act and the whole world could see it thereafter. Celebrities around the world are afraid of the camera when it comes to the display of negative things.

In the glare of the public, everybody behaves as an angel, but in the absence of the multitude, many people show their true self, by displaying the evil in them. Only the fear of God is the remedy for this absurdity. Oh! That all men will know that we are living our lives under God's camera! When Judas perfected his plans to betray Jesus, he could not carry out the nefarious act in the glare of everybody.

"And he promised, and sought opportunity to betray him unto them in the absence of the multitude" Luke. 22: 6.

The absence of the multitude is a good opportunity for those who do not have the fear of God to manifest their real nature. However, the fear of God reminds us that God's camera is permanently beamed on our lives even when no one is watching.

The Fear of Man

There are at least three kinds of fear: the fear of man, the fear of the unknown and the fear of God. Out of these three categories of fear, the fear of man is the worst. While the fear of God perfects holiness, the fear of the unknown creates anxiety and the fear of man brings bondage.

In the words of Jesus to us, He admonishes us to rather fear God who can destroy both body and soul than to fear man who can only destroy the physical body (Matt. 10: 28). While the fear of God is the beginning of wisdom, the fear of the unknown is the onset of anxiety and the fear of man is an invitation to slavery.

Reading between the lines of the words of Jesus in Matthew 10:26- 28, He does not expect us to fear man. It does not mean in any way that we should not respect man, but it means in every way that we should not be cowed. There are certain people in this 21st century, who believe in the word of Jesus that they must be born again, but they are not able to do so because of the fear of man. Some of them show more courage by giving their lives to Christ secretly. A married woman gave her life to Christ secretly and was practicing Christianity for a while without her husband and close associates knowing. After a while, her husband also gave his life to Christ secretly. He hid his faith in Christ for sometimes. One day he summoned up courage to tell his wife about his new found faith. To his surprise, his wife narrated her encounter with Christ and that brought an end to their mutual fear.

The Bible did not leave us without a clear understanding of the fact that both the fear of man and fear of the unknown have torments (1 Jn. 4: 18). In fact, when Paul was writing to Timothy, his son in the faith, he told him plainly what God has not given to us.

"For God hath not given us the spirit of fear; but of power, and of love, and of a sound mind" 2 Tim. 1: 7.

There is a revelation in this Scriptures; and it is that fear is a spirit. Fear is a spirit, but it is not a good spirit. Remember, in this context the fear that the Bible is talking about is not the fear of God. This is an important note, because there is a spirit called "The spirit of the fear of God". This is one of the components of the seven-fold Spirit of God. This spirit has the capacity to make a believer of quick understanding in the fear of the LORD (Isaiah 11: 13).

"And the spirit of the LORD shall rest upon him, the spirit of wisdom and understanding, the spirit of counsel and might, the spirit of knowledge and of the fear of the LORD" Isaiah 11: 2.

In the Amplified version, the last part is rendered "reverential and obedient fear of the Lord". This is a prophetic Scripture about the Lord Jesus Christ and by extension; it applies to the believer in Christ. So, we see clearly that there are two spirits of fear: the spirit of the fear of man and of the unknown on one hand, and the spirit of the fear of God on the other hand. Of course, the two spirits here are in different classes. The former is negative and destructive, while the latter is positive and constructive. Again, while the former is satanically induced, the latter is God ordained. There is no greater freedom than that a man overcomes the spirit of fear and becomes possessed by the spirit of the fear of the LORD.

Kept by His Fear

"By mercy and truth iniquity is purged: and by the fear of the LORD men depart from evil" Proverbs 16: 6.

It is not in man that lives in the world to keep himself from sin, but for the fear of the Lord. When we go back to the story of Joseph and his encounter with Portipher's wife, the only reason why a young man will reject the invitation of his mistress, lose his garment, just to preserve his godly character is the deep rooted reverential fear of God in his heart. The contrast between the life of Joseph and of Samson is very pronounced.

While the principled Joseph was constrained from evil by the fear of God, the anointed Samson was scintillated by women in the absence of the fear of God.

Daniel was among those who were taken captive and became slaves in Babylon. He had lived all his life as a Jew in Israel until they went into captivity. When he was in this strange land of Babylon he was introduced to a new lifestyle. But Daniel purposed in his heart that he would not defile himself in the new environment he found himself (Dan. 1: 1-8). It is clear from studies that his determination not to defile himself was a wisdom which was propelled by the fear of God. Come to think of it, if Daniel had decided to change his lifestyle in Babylon, not many people would have known about it. Of course, it is easy to justify such a change of life style. One would have said, "He is not like that, it is his environment that affected him". But the fear of God inscribed in the heart of Daniel would not allow him to become an 'environmental Christian'.

I met a Ghanaian woman whom I took as a mother some years ago in Austria. We were attending an International Pentecostal Church together at that time. She narrated a painful story of some Ghanaians that she knew as Christians back in her home country. Some of them made their way to Austria and Germany. Not long after these Ghanaians got to stay in their host countries, their lives completely changed to reflect their new environment.

They were into all kinds of unprintable things. They abandoned God to the point that even Church attendance was no longer on their list of things to do. Their new environment simply swallowed them up because the fear of God was not deeply rooted in them. When the fear of God is not in place, the tendency is high that men will change in tune with their environment and the circumstances of life.

Solomon wrote to his son and said, *"My son, if sinners entice thee, consent thou not. If they say, come with us, let us lay wait for blood, let us lurk privily for the innocent without cause: Let us swallow them up alive as the grave; and whole, as those that go down into the pit: We shall find all precious substance, we shall fill our houses with spoil: Cast in thy lot among us; let us all have one purse: My son, walk not thou in the way with them; refrain thy foot from their path"* Prov. 1: 10-15.

This Wisdom of Solomon will be a mere advice without the fear of God in the heart of his son. One of the greatest responsibilities that parents have towards their children is to instill the fear of the Lord in their hearts. When we prayerfully teach our children about God, His requirements and His judgments, the chances are high that the fear of God will be entrenched in them. This is what will keep the children from doing things which dishonour God and such things that bring shame to parents.

Benefits of His Fear

When people understand what they stand to benefit in any endeavour, they naturally become more committed to it. The fear of God has benefits. It is actually in our best interest to fear the Lord.

"The fear of the Lord tendeth to life: and he that hath it shall abide satisfied; he shall not be visited with evil" Prov. 19: 23.

The three fold blessings enumerated as a product of the fear of the Lord, form the basic aspiration of the human race in all generations. A sensible human being wants to live and not die. He does not only want to live, he wants to be satisfied and he wants evil to be far from him.

When we begin to walk in the fear of the Lord, these three blessings will naturally follow us. It is okay to pray for long life, it is not bad to ask God to satisfy you, neither is it wrong to pray against evil in one's life; but all these prayers could be answered in one act of wisdom - Fear the Lord.

"He who fears the LORD has a secure fortress, and for his children it will be a refuge. The fear of the Lord is a fountain of life, turning a man from the snares of death" Prov. 14: 26-27 NIV.

Two thieves were nailed to the cross with Jesus at Calvary. Shortly before their death, they manifested their character (Luke. 23: 39-45). While one of the thieves accused Jesus of not saving Himself and saving them as well, the other thief recognized the missing element in his colleague, *"...Dost not thou fear God, seeing thou art in the same condemnation?"* vs. 40. Invariably, one of the thieves had not the fear of God while the other had the fear of God. The difference between the two of them became clear at the end of the day. While the one without the fear of God died, the one with the fear of God was turned from the snares of death when Jesus said, unto him, *"verily I say unto thee, Today shalt thou be with me in paradise"* vs. 43. Oh how true it is, *"The fear of the Lord is a fountain of life, turning a man from the snares of death"* Prov. 14: 27 NIV.

Oh! That man will fear the Lord for His wonderful works and all the blessings which are embedded therein.

Chapter Seven

A Deeper Life with God

CHRISTIANITY IS NOT A CALL TO a shallow experience; it is rather a call to swim in the deep ocean of God's love. If we choose to swim on the surface of the mighty waters, we will loose the essence of the call. Let's take the fishing experience of Peter in Luke chapter five as an analogy of the Christian faith. Peter, according to his testimony had toiled all night and caught nothing. Then Jesus showed up at the point that he was washing his net. In an attempt to prove to Peter that the same instruments could produce a different result, Jesus began with borrowing his boat. After using Peter's boat as a platform to teach the word, He then instructed Peter to launch into the deep for a catch. Apparently, before the instruction to launch into the deep, Peter was fishing on the shallow side of the water. Could this explain why he caught nothing on this occasion? Possibly!

Now, the same net which Peter used before the instruction came from Jesus, was what he used after the instruction. The same instrument produced a different result. Two factors could have been responsible for this. The first is the instruction that Jesus gave. This is true because results are a direct product of God's instruction. The second factor is that the net was launched into the deep. The probability of catching fish on surface water is nearly zero. Normally, in any sphere of life, the deeper you go the better it is. The believer, who specializes on surface relationship with God and expects results, may have to wait for a long time for it, if there would be any result at all.

Why do some people think Christianity is not anything worthwhile? The answer could be that they have not gone beyond surface analysis of it. If you try to classify Christianity among the religions of the world, it will fail the test required for such classification. The strength of Christianity does not lie in observing a set of rules, as it is in other religions, but it lies in a deep rooted relationship with the Saviour of the world. And it gets better as the relationship gets deeper. Just as Peter got results when he launched into the deep water, so does every believer who launches into a deep spiritual relationship with the Father of all spirits.

It's amazing the kind of results a believer can produce if he gets deeper in the things of God. The deep things of God are reserved for those who have a deep relationship with Him. This is captured in the popular statement, "the deep calls unto the deep." (Ps.42:7)

The Knowledge of God

"And such as do wickedly against the covenant shall he corrupt by flatteries: but the people that do know their God shall be strong, and do exploits" Dan. 11: 32.

Being strong and doing exploits are a result of a continuous knowledge of God. It is not enough to know God at the point of salvation, you must move on from there in a progressive way. The basic knowledge which people have about God may not be enough for a life of distinction. There is the need to continuously avail ourselves to know more of Him. When we sit down to study the Bible, we make ourselves available to know Him. The first point of call in the knowledge of God is the most holy book, the Bible.

The Berea Christians were a special group of believers because they paid attention to the Bible (Acts 17: 11). Each time they attended a Church service, they listened to the word and went back home to re-examine it to see if it aligns with Scriptures. Once there is no alignment of what they have received with the Bible, they will discard it and cling to what the Bible says. Such is the attitude of all those who are committed to the knowledge of God. They would not work with just what the pastor says, but what God says as revealed in Scriptures. In other words, if there is a conflict between what the pastor says with what the Bible says, they will go for what the Bible says and let go of what the pastor had said.

The book of Daniel 11: 32 can be rendered conversely to produce a different, but true meaning: "The people that do not know their God shall be weak and be exploited". Often times, the devil capitalizes on the weakness of men to floor them. Assuredly, the weaknesses of men are enhanced by their ignorance of God. Therefore, the devil's old tricks have been to keep men away from the knowledge of God, so that he could have a vulnerable group of people who could be manipulated easily. When Jesus confronted a group of people who were in error, He identified ignorance as the culprit: "...*ye do err, not knowing the scriptures nor the power of God*" (Matt. 22: 29).

Jehovah's lamentation over His people in the book of Hosea was that of ignorance: "*My people are destroyed for lack of knowledge: because thou hast rejected knowledge, I will also reject thee, that thou shalt be no more priest to me: seeing thou hast forgotten the law of thy God, I will also forget thy children*" Hosea 4: 6.

Ignorance is the background on which the devil operates to unleash destruction on the children of men. Unfortunately, the devil's operation could even affect the people of God who are ignorant of God's provisions in His word. Thus says the Lord, "the only way out of destruction is the knowledge of God".

In this era of knowledge, people have paid attention to many areas. The internet has opened up a new vista for knowledge; satellite communications have made significant contributions. New frontiers of knowledge are being advanced by the day. By the way, all of these advancements in knowledge that we see in our world today, are a long time predictions of the Bible. God had shown to Daniel that towards the end of time, people shall run to and fro and knowledge shall be increased (Dan. 12: 4). This is exactly what is happening today. There has been so much of running 'to and fro' in confusion. People are running from pillar to post not knowing what to do in handling terrorism. Of course, knowledge has so much increased that one wonders if there is nothing the world has not already known by now. This fulfillment of prophecy which is outside the scope of this book authenticates the Bible as the authority on which to base the knowledge of God.

With the growing body of knowledge in the world today, I am concerned that not everybody is paying attention to the knowledge of God. Agreed, not everybody will naturally pay attention to the knowledge of God. But if more people get to know more things outside of the knowledge of God, the world can not be better for it. This explains why despite so much knowledge, we have more problems that look insurmountable. In the face of all these knowledge, there is a deficit of God's knowledge. Know for sure that once the knowledge of God is in short supply in a given society, the societal problems are set to multiply. What we need is the knowledge of God and of the things around us in a balanced proportion.

A Heart Cry

"(For my determined purpose is) that I may know Him (that I may progressively become more deeply and intimately acquainted with Him, perceiving and recognizing and understanding the wonders of His Person more strongly and more clearly), and that I may in that same way come to know the power outflowing from His resurrection (which it exerts over believers), and that I may so share His sufferings as to be continually transformed (in spirit into His likeness even) to His death, (in the hope). That if possible I may attain to the (spiritual and moral) resurrection (that lifts me) out from among the dead (even while in the body)" Phil 3: 10-11 AMP.

Hidden in these verses of Scriptures is one of the secrets of the successful life that Paul the apostle lived. When Paul the apostle was an unbeliever, he pursued knowledge until he became a successful lawyer (Phil. 3: 4-8). Perhaps, one of the attributes which God was interested in Paul's life before He got him converted was his quest for knowledge. His salvation experience did not quench his thirst for knowledge; it only shifted its focus. So, we see Paul the apostle expressing his desire for the knowledge of God. He puts his desire as "My determined purpose".

Let me pause to ask you an important question of life: what is your determined purpose? At least two persons have the answer. First, God knows your determined purpose. Second, you know your determined purpose. Your determined purpose is your defining adjective. Some people's determined purpose is money; and they pursue it to a fault. For others, their determined purpose is fame. Somebody once said, "The world must know me". I hope the world knows him for good. This is important because some people are famous on the wrong side of history.

Importantly, our determined purpose should be like that of Paul: "that we may progressively become more deeply and intimately acquainted with Him, perceiving and recognizing and understanding the wonders of His Person more strongly and more clearly". What can be more than this? No matter the pursuit of life, ultimate fulfillment lies in the pursuit of a higher purpose - the knowledge of God! The basic truth is that until you know God, you don't know anything. We must learn to cry after the knowledge of God, as a baby cries for milk when hungry.

Hunger and Thirst after Righteousness

In life, what we pursue is what we may likely get. Those who pursue a career in sports may end up becoming stars, while those who pursue a career in the academia may end up as professors. In the same vein, if you follow after righteousness you are well on track to achieving it. In the words of Jesus He says, *"Blessed are they which do hunger and thirst after righteousness: for they shall be filled"* Matt. 5: 6.

The secret of a life filled with righteousness, is a hunger and a thirst for it. For human beings, hunger and thirst is a common denominator. Everybody is prone to it at one time or the other. When you see a hungry man, it tells on him. Without food and water, the human race will be completely wiped out in a matter of weeks. That underscores the importance of food and water to the physical well being of humans.

As food and water is to the physical body, so is righteousness to the spiritual life. There is no true spirituality without righteousness. As a matter of fact, without righteousness the spiritual life famishes and remains starved of vitality.

The reason why the body hungers and thirsts for food and water is because these two ingredients are essential to the human body. Similarly, the reason why Jesus demands we should hunger and thirst after righteousness, is because it is essential for our spiritual well being.

For the believer in Christ, a continuous hunger and thirst after righteousness culminates in a deeper life with the Almighty. The assurance which Jesus gives in the above Scripture is that, if the hunger and thirst is a continuum, and the goal is righteousness, then the end result will be a spiritual satisfaction.

Enlarge Yourself

A glass cup that contains water to the brim is said to be filled. So also, a bucket containing water to its brim is said to be filled. Both containers can be said to be filled with water, but their capacity is not the same. Even though, the glass cup is filled with water, if by any means it were possible for it to be enlarged, it will have more space to take more water. When we gave our lives to Christ and received the baptism of the Holy Spirit, we became filled with the Spirit of God. But what we were filled with at baptism is not all that there is in God. We can take in more of God depending on our capacities. What you need in order to have more of God is an enlarged capacity.

How do we then enlarge ourselves in the things of God? The answer is in Hosea 10: 12, *"Sow to yourselves in righteousness, reap in mercy; break up your fallow ground: for it is time to seek the LORD, till he come and rain righteousness upon you"*. Often times, when we successfully enlarge ourselves for more of God, He comes around to rain righteousness upon us. To the prepared heart, God always comes not in dew, but in a rain. Remember that the rain is the symbol of God's blessing to the earth. It is the rain that determines the earth's productivity. When the rain comes to the earth, it waters it, makes it to bring forth and gives food to its inhabitants (Isaiah 55: 10). So, the rain of God upon a man is actually a baptism of blessing. May the God of Heaven rain righteousness upon you.

Just as there are two sides to a coin, so also there are two sides to God's covenant. When God makes a promise, He gives you your own side of the bargain. There is no blessing of God that gets to you without responsibility. The three responsibilities placed on us from Hosea 10: 12 are: sow to yourselves in righteousness, reap in mercy, and break up your follow ground.

In His wisdom, God designed life to be all about sowing and reaping. The seeds you sow today, determines what you harvest tomorrow. Hear the wisdom, sow to yourself in righteousness today and by tomorrow you will reap in God's mercy.

However, sowing and reaping is preceded by breaking up your fallow ground. A fallow ground is an uncultivated ground. Before a farmer goes to plant seeds, he prepares the ground. Part of the preparation includes the breaking of an uncultivated ground. The preparation of our hearts before God in order to carry a new level of grace is what it means to break up our uncultivated ground. It includes but not limited to our waiting upon the Lord to renew our strength. As believers, we must constantly look at an uncultivated area of our lives and break it up, sow seeds in righteousness and expect the harvest in God's mercy. By so doing, we will constantly enlarge ourselves for more of God in our lives.

Ask for His Presence

The deeper life is characterized by His presence in our lives. When a believer's highest pursuit in life is to carry the divine presence, he has just elected to be numbered among the great. Moses the man of God refused to embark on any journey without the presence of God. The Bible has the record of an interesting conversation between God and Moses about the divine presence: *"The LORD replied, my presence will go with you, and I will give you rest. Then Moses said to him, if your presence does not go with us, do not send us up from here"* Exodus. 33: 14-15 NIV.

Clearly speaking, the above Scripture points to the fact that there is always a convergence of the divine presence and true rest. To underscore the premium that Moses placed on the presence of God, as soon as God promised to go with him, he quickly insisted before the Almighty that God's presence is the precondition for their journey. If we can all come to terms with the assurance of His presence, the journey of life will be a walk over. Obviously, Heaven's commitment to our successful journey in life was what made Jesus to promise us the divine presence. The last statement from the mouth of Jesus to His disciples before His departure is very powerful as a guarantee for a smooth sail through life: *"... And surely I am with you always, to the very end of the age"* Matt. 28: 20 NIV.

Normally, when people are given an assignment, they negotiate with the giver of the assignment on what they need in order to carry out a successful job. For Solomon whom God made king over Israel, he asked God for wisdom to do the assignment (1 Kings. 3: 5-13). For

Gideon, he asked God for a sign (Judges 6: 14-22). But for Moses the friend of God, he asked for the presence of the possessor of Heaven and earth. There is great wisdom in the request of Moses. This is because the presence of God gives direction, it gives confidence, it removes fear and it defeats the enemy.

To constantly secure the presence of God, we must seek always to do the things that please Him. If the pleasure of God becomes our daily desire, then our lives become so attractive to God that He literally comes to make His abode in us. Jesus alluded to this fact when He said, "...*The father hath not left me alone, for I do always those things that please him*" (Jn. 8: 29). If you please Him, you will attract Him. Have you not noticed that your life becomes attractive to the people that you please? Of course, that is how it works; any child who pleases his parents will get their attention whenever he needs them. The principle of God's attraction is embedded in a lifestyle of His pleasure. What is the prayer point here? The prayer is simple. Dear Lord, help me to make my life such a pleasure to You, a sweet smelling savour, so that I can attract You to my life on a daily basis. This should constantly be the prayer of a man who does not want to step out of the boundary of a deeper relationship with God.

Chapter Eight

Let's Talk About Integrity

BACK IN AFRICA WHERE MONEY IS transferred from the central bank to other commercial banks in a physical manner, it is normal to see a bullion van conveying money from time to time with a police escort. The question is why does the transfer of money require police escort? The answer is that the society places high value on money. If there is no such police escort, there is the likelihood of somebody or some people hijacking the money on transit in a 'commando' style operation. Let's think for a moment, "what if there is a van full of integrity to be conveyed from one city to another?" Will it require a police escort? It is doubtful. This is because the society does not place much value on integrity. But the truth is we need integrity in every facet of our lives.

When I closed my eyes to imagine a society which needs no policing, I found a society called the 'integral society'. This society values integrity above money. It believes that there is more to success than just winning at all cost. This society believes that one should have a sense of fair play at the end of every endeavour. This same society reserves the highest honour in the land not to the rich, but to men who are of honest report. There was not a single policeman in that society which I saw in my imagination. What a society! It looks actually like an ideal society. Of course, when I opened my eyes, I saw a real society that is way off from the ideal. Then I began to wish that the real society will work towards the ideal. But mere wishes cannot make it happen. What the real society needs to attain the ideal is a conscious effort to de-emphasize the craze for money, and re-emphasize integrity as a top-rated virtue. A life lived with integrity, even if it is devoid of fame and fortune, is worthy of honour.

Men of Honest Report

Not many days after the day of Pentecost, when the power of the Holy Ghost came upon the Church, it grew astronomically. The growth was something in the range of some thousands. Of course, this growth came with challenges. There were complaints of neglect in the daily distribution of food between the Grecians and the Hebrews. True to type, anywhere you find people and there are scarce resources, there is bound to be complaints in its distribution. So, the apostles responded to the crisis by appointing leaders who could solve the problem (Acts 6; 1-6). The interesting thing is that they chose not just men who were full of the Holy Ghost and wisdom, but men of honest report; men of impeccable character! A man of integrity has a report card of honesty by the people among whom he lives.

My guess is that the task of finding seven men who had three sterling qualities combined was a serious research work. The Bible did not tell us how long it took to find these men that assumed the leadership position which further enhanced the growth of the Church. But it could be reasonably assumed that it was not a day's job. If the apostles could wait to appoint the right men despite the urgency of the problem, it tells you the importance which they placed on qualification.

Interestingly, the first qualification that the apostles expected to be on the deacons' curriculum vitae was 'men of honest report', which is synonymous with men of integrity. But why didn't they ask for the most spiritual quality of being "full of the Holy Ghost"? It is because men could be full of the Holy Ghost and yet lack integrity. We have seen tongue talking believers who stole public funds. If the apostles had not factored in the issue of integrity, it would have been possible to find one or two deacon(s) who could embezzle some of the food which were being distributed, and thereby worsening the problem. With integrity, the ministry is saved from the greed of its leaders.

The Principle of Fair Play

The story was told of a Director who took his car to have it repaired. He searched for an honest mechanic and he had one recommended to him. The mechanic started work on the Director's car and spent three hours without being able to fix it. After those long hours of fruitless labour, he confessed to the Director his inability to fix the car. Reluctantly, the car owner asked the mechanic how much will he collect for his efforts. Surprisingly, the mechanic refused to accept money for the car he could not fix. Stunned by the mechanic's gesture, the Director saw a hero in him. But this was the daily lifestyle of the mechanic, as his neighbours testified. He had a commitment to make an honest living.

The practice of the above mechanic has its root in Scriptures which says, *"Live such good lives among the pagans that, though they accuse you of doing wrong, they may see your good deeds and glorify God on the day he visits us"* 1 Pet. 2: 12 NIV.

There is no need getting money that you have not earned, except if it is a gift. Of course, if the Director had decided to go ahead and give some money to the mechanic, it becomes a gift. If it is not a gift, then make sure you earn your living. For a man of integrity, a dollar earned is far more than five found.

It is difficult to believe that Jacob dealt fairly with his father-in-law, when he practiced the negative principle of wealth transfer. Which ever way you look at it, Jacob had an ulterior motive while he negotiated with his father-in-law over his wages (Gen. 30: 27- 43). And, whenever there is an ulterior motive in any dealing, integrity is compromised.

The reason why Jacob could not apply the principle of fair play in his dealing with Laban, was due largely to the fact that he was too selfish to be considerate. To the degree that a man expresses his selfish nature, to that degree he loses integrity. That is to say, integrity is inversely proportional to selfishness. Often times, selfishness manifests itself as greed. It is my believe that if the nature of selfishness as manifested in greed is conquered, the world will have a sigh of relieve from her oppressors.

The Leadership Question

It is true that vision forms one of the most cardinal qualities of a successful leader. Following closely however, is the issue of integrity. A visionary leader who lacks integrity will soon lose followership. While vision could determine a man's success, integrity sustains it. Think about a corporate organization, like a bank, that has a very great vision. Such an organization will surely attract so many customers in just a moment. But having subjected the bank to integrity test by the customers and it fails, the bank will loose its customers at the same rate that it gained them.

For a minister of the gospel, the anointing can attract men to the ministry, but integrity is needed to keep the men within the ministry. Most important decisions which men take revolve around integrity. If people cannot trust you, they can't commit anything serious into your hands. When Jesus was dying on the cross of Calvary, He committed His spirit to God's hands (Luke. 23: 46). He did this as a demonstration of His trust in God. The soul of Jesus was too precious to let go, without committing it to the One who is trustworthy. Ironically, however, some people commit their lives to the devil that cannot be trusted. It is such a waste of life to commit anything to the devil. The devil is not a man of integrity, so he cannot be a good leader. At best he is a gangster, so don't follow him.

Looking down memory lane, I fondly remembered my elementary school days. I just pictured myself on the assembly line some thirty four years back, singing a popular song that they used to teach us: "wherever you go, wherever you be, do not say yes when you mean to say no". What a lesson on integrity communicated to elementary school children in a song, in those days! How I wish this song will come up on national and international television, to teach the adults of this generation the basics of integrity.

It appears as if the missing link in leaders of today is this issue of integrity. The question is, "can a leader be blameless?" Yes, if integrity is in place. But does it mean he cannot make mistakes? No, he can make mistakes because he is human. By our make up as humans, mistakes are probable. The fact is that lack of integrity is not the same thing as a mistake. While lack of integrity is a serious issue, a mistake may be a trivial matter. A lack of integrity could lead to a criminal offence, but a mistake is forgivable. While a lack of integrity is a character problem, a mistake is an occurrence that may never re-occur. Without integrity, leadership is a play. According to Ziglar, "the most important persuasion tool you have in your entire arsenal is integrity". People will likely follow you when you have shown yourself to them as an example.

David asked questions about the qualifications of those who can abide in the tabernacle of the Lord. And he went ahead to provide the answers to the questions he asked. Let's look at the questions and the answers in Psalms 15.

"O LORD, who may abide in your tent? Who may dwell on Your holy hill? He who walks with integrity, and works righteousness, And speaks truth in his heart" Ps. 15: 1-2 NAS.

Wow! What an answer. Integrity is the first qualification that is mentioned in the above Scripture. For it to be mentioned first in the list of qualifications is to underscore the importance of integrity. Remember, David was asking for qualifications that associate us with God. No man can keep his association with God that is not a man of integrity. If I am to ask one of the questions which David asked, I will say, "Lord, can a bishop abide in your tabernacle?" Following the pattern of David's answer, I could also provide the answer to my question thus: "Yes, if the bishop is a man of integrity". With integrity in place, all other qualifications listed in Psalms 15 will naturally fit in.

Not only will a man of integrity work righteousness, he will speak the truth from his heart. Part of his integrity involves neither slandering with his tongue nor doing evil to his neighbour. The honour that a man of integrity gives is not to vile persons but to those who fear the Lord. It is integrity for a man to keep his oath even when it hurts. A man of integrity can give out his money without expectation of any profit, neither does he accept bribe to thwart judgment. The qualification needed to dwell with God is all about integrity.

Are You Transparent?

A transparent person is one that anybody can see through. To be transparent is to have no secret dealings. This surely is an aspect of integrity. When a man is transparent, he has no skeleton in his cupboard. Jacob served his father in law for twenty years. The first seven years was for his interchanged wife, Leah. The next seven years was for his beloved, but delayed wife, Rachael. Of course, the last six years was for economic gain. Finally, he made up his mind to return to his home country. He picked his wives, children and wealth to go back home (Gen. 31: 14-55). The query to Jacob is, "why do you leave your father-in-law's house secretly?" Whenever there is secrecy in any dealing, there is no transparency. If there was no skeleton in Jacob's cupboard, he would have told his father-in-law of his departure.

Well, unfortunately for Laban, even his own daughter had a secret dealing with him. Rachael stole his gods. It is laughable that some people's gods can be stolen. How do you serve a god that cannot protect himself from robbers? Anyway, when Rachael stole her father's gods, she hid them in the camel's furniture and sat on them. Again, imagine a god that one can sit on. It is primitive to serve such kind of god. The point however, is that just like Jacob; Rachael was not transparent in her dealing with her father. She kept the gods away from the glare of her father, with the pretence that she was going through her period. All un-transparent people are pretenders. They do one thing in the secret, and show the world a different picture. God hates this kind of dual posture so He says, *"And have no fellowship with the unfruitful works of darkness, but rather reprove them. For it is a shame even to speak of those things which are done of them in secret. But all things that are reproved are made manifest by the light: for whatsoever doth make manifest is light"* Eph. 5: 11-13.

What is God saying? Have no relationship with anything that is done in the secret, but rather make your life such an example of transparency to the intent that you will reprove the secrecy of men.

Being True to Yourself

In the final analysis, your choices and decisions are what determine your happiness in life. Doing the right thing so that it sits comfortably with one's self is ultimately the important criteria in personal integrity. You should know when you have done the right thing. The highest disservice you can do is to tell yourself a lie. If a man succeeds in deceiving himself, he has no man left to deceive.

When Paul was concluding his letter to the Corinthian Church, he told them clearly that they have a responsibility to be true to themselves.

"Examine yourselves, whether ye be in the faith; prove your own selves. Know ye not your own selves, how that Jesus Christ is in you, except ye be reprobates?" 2 Cor. 13: 5.

The power lies within us to know how we have fared in all our endeavours. Unfortunately, when a man suppresses the truth about himself, he loses the opportunity to express what is called personal integrity. No matter how much it hurts when confronted with your true state, accept it and make the necessary change as a way of being remorseful and true to yourself.

The Practice of Integrity

Over the years men have come to realize that there is a gap between theory and practice. The theory is needed to give a better understanding of the practice. But the theory alone cannot lead to the practice. It takes a whole lot of determination to translate theory into practice. The best way to live a life of integrity is to step into its practice. This may even begin in small ways such as keeping to time. It is said that practice makes perfect. If this is a true statement, it means that as you step into the practice of integrity, you are on your way to perfection. It is even possible to fail on some occasions, but if you are not deterred in your commitment to live a life of integrity, you will soon reach the promised land.

The life of integrity may come through many years of working hard on it. Integrity is like building an edifice, it cannot be a one day affair. It is said that Rome was not built in a day. It is easier to build cities or nations than to build integrity. While cities or nations can be built over a period of time, integrity requires a lifetime to build. Live your life on a daily basis working on integrity until you see Jesus. Have the courage to say no when it is the right thing to do so. Receive the courage to face the truth. Do the right thing because it is right. These are the magic keys to living your life with integrity.

Chapter Nine

The Crucified Life

"I am crucified with Christ: nevertheless I live, yet not I, but Christ liveth in me: and the life which I now live in the flesh I live by the faith of the Son of God, who loved me, and gave himself for me" Gal. 2: 20.

ABOUT TWO DECADES AGO WHEN SOME of us gave our lives to Christ, this Scripture was our guiding principle. We sang such songs as, "It is no longer I that liveth, but Christ that liveth in me". I personally was propelled to live for Christ by all means in the light of this Scripture.

Today, we must re-emphasize the crucified life if we must live for Christ. It is not enough to be born again, but to walk in the consciousness of the crucified life. Without the crucified life, a believer is tempted to choose the easy road as a way out of trouble. Jesus said there are two ways in life: the broad way and the narrow way (Matt. 7: 13-14). These two ways have their destinations. The broad way leads to hell and destruction, while the narrow way leads to Heaven.

These two ways have their characteristics: The broad way has many people on it, while the narrow way has few people on it. What this means is that there are more easy loving people than those who can make a sacrifice for the kingdom. It takes the crucified life to choose the narrow way.

Crucifixion is synonymous with pain. So, a crucified man can take a painful decision in favour of Christ. When Peter denied Jesus at a crucial hour of his life, it was a simple indication that Peter could not take a painful decision in favour of Christ.

When Jesus was crucified on the cross, He literally died. So when we say we are crucified with Him, we are saying that we died. Of course, the secret of life in Christ is death to self. There is no man who is alive in Christ today that did not first die. You will notice in the above verse of Scripture which the apostle Paul wrote to the Galatians, that he did not talk about the life of Christ in him, before talking of his crucifixion with Christ. This suggests that the crucified life is the means to the life of Christ.

The Lust of the Eyes

If everybody in the world was to be blind, there probably would have been fewer problems in the world today. For sure, blindness is a major problem that can take its toll on the world's economy. But I made this statement because of the reality that many of our problems are caused by what we see. The pornographic industry has polluted much of the world's population because of what they make people to see. The crazy dressings that we see around us today have a sex appeal to the eyes. If men were blind, ladies will not need to wear seductive clothes.

When John was writing as a father to his children, he said to them: *"Love not the world, neither the things that are in the world, if any man love the world, the love of the Father is not in him. For all that is in the world, the lust of the flesh, and the lust of the eyes, and the pride of life, is not of the Father, but is of the world"* 1 Jn. 2: 15-16.

Clearly, the lust of the eyes is one component of the world that has made people captives of sin. The eye is a powerful gateway through which evil can gain entrance. When the eyes receive pictures, the heart processes them. When Eve was tempted by the devil in the Garden of Eden, her eyes were very instrumental to her fall.

"And when the woman saw that the tree was good for food, and that it was pleasant to the eyes, and a tree to be desired to make one wise, she took of the fruit thereof, and did eat, and gave also unto her husband with her; and he did eat" Gen. 3: 6.

To walk by sight is to move in the direction of temptation, and no man who walks in that direction is spared from sin. The failure of Lot was partly caused by what he saw. Abraham and Lot his nephew had dwelt together for long until God's prosperity brought about a separation. As they were ready to part ways, Lot made a costly mistake simply because he made a choice by sight. He lifted up his eyes and saw the plain of Jordan, that it was green and luring. But the problem with the garden which he saw was that it was in a bad location; it was toward Sodom (Gen. 13: 5-13). Lot did not mind its location, because it was appealing to the eyes. It is almost, always a horrible mistake for a believer to act based on what he sees with the physical eyes. The Scripture says; *"For we walk by faith, not by sight"* (2 Cor. 5: 7). The good news is that for the man who is crucified with Christ, his eyes are closed to the world and its appealing pleasures.

The Pride of Life

When the devil came to tempt Jesus, he appealed to Him in three areas: First, the lust of the flesh; when he asked Jesus to turn stone to bread so that Jesus could satisfy Himself. Second, the pride of life; when the devil took Jesus to the pinnacle and asked Him to show to the world who He is, by casting Himself down, so that angels could bear Him up as a sign that He is the Son of God. Third, the lust of the eyes; when the devil showed Jesus the glory of the world and promised to give it to Jesus in exchange for worship (Matt. 4: 1-11). Is it not funny that the devil was courageous enough to tempt the Master in such a comprehensive way?

The pride of life is displayed in men each time they try to show who they are. The tragedy is that many people do not display who they are in Christ, but who they are in the world.

The story was told of a couple that was invited to attend a wedding. Unfortunately, the wedding card for the invited couple did not carry their proper title. It was addressed as, 'Mr. and Mrs.' instead of 'Dr and Mrs.' This couple insisted that the invitation card be corrected to reflect their status as a pre-condition for them to attend the wedding. Without an iota of doubt, this is a manifestation of the pride of life. In today's world of class, some people cannot marry from a particular family no matter the conviction. Others cannot associate with some group of people that they consider inferior.

The pride of life often manifests itself in what is called 'superiority complex'. Even in Church, some people have a 'holier than thou' attitude. All through the ministry of Jesus on earth, the Pharisees could not understand why He talked, ate and related with sinners freely. However, the mystery of the gospel is that Christ came to the earth so as to reconcile sinful men to the 'thrice' Holy God. Whatever is the reputation of a believer, the crucified life helps to set it aside in order to live a simple life for Christ's sake.

The Lust of the Flesh

The flesh will always betray its followers unless it is crucified. Why is it difficult for some people to fast when they should? The straight answer is the flesh tells them otherwise. Those who are called gluttons are people whose appetite for food has taken a good part of them. For the believer who finds himself in this class, the consciousness of the crucified life can nail the affection for food to the cross.

Esau would not have sold his birthright to Jacob his brother, if not for food problem (Gen. 25: 27-34). Maybe if Esau was able to defer his hunger by one hour, the story would have been different. All that Esau needed to do was to manage to enter the kitchen and prepare his own meal. One hour would have been enough to prepare something to eat. Regrettably, his flesh cost him his future. When the flesh is not crucified, the future is mortgaged.

At the time that the devil tempted Jesus to turn stone to bread just to satisfy the flesh, Jesus had answer for him.

"...It is written, man shall not live by bread alone, but by every word that proceedeth out of the mouth of God" Matt. 4: 4.

It is my prayer that the believer will always have an answer for the devil from God's word, each time he comes to tempt us to drift from the truth.

What we need to eat, to drink and to wear are all materials for the flesh. But the Bible says we should not be carried away by these things, because the Father knows that we have need of these things (Matt. 6: 31-33). The beauty of the crucified life is that, it redirects our minds to the things of God, away from the things that the world focuses on.

Daily Cross Bearing

I have watched with amazement many people who have a cross on their necks as part of their dress code. It may be a good way to remember that the Christian life is a call to daily cross bearing. Sadly however, some of the people who wear the cross live their lives in contrast with the cross. It is not the cross on a man, but a man on the cross that matters.

Jesus did not leave His disciples without telling them the hard truth: *"And he said to them all, if any man will come after me, let him deny himself, and take up his cross daily, and follow me"* Luke. 9: 23.

The life of cross bearing is a life of self-denial. Preparatory to the crucifixion of Jesus on the cross of Calvary, a man of Cyrene by name Simon was compelled to bear the physical cross on which Jesus was to be crucified (Matt. 27: 31-32). This man had no option at that time, because it was forced on him. In contemporary times, no body can be forced to carry the cross. It is a decision to be taken out of self-will. As a matter of fact, Jesus demands that every one should take up his cross daily and follow the Master. In plain language, there is no need following the Master without a cross. You must remember that the cross is a symbol of sacrifice. So, when Jesus was talking of carrying the cross, it was a figurative expression for the life of sacrifice. Christianity was actually born out of sacrifice, propagated by sacrifice and can only be sustained by sacrifice. Any believer that evades the daily sacrificial life of Christianity should as well forget about its attendant glory that is to come in the next life.

Christian Fruitfulness

Fruitfulness in spiritual things lies in the proverbial corn of wheat falling to the ground and dying. In actual sense, life begins with death.

"Verily, verily, I say unto you, Except a corn of wheat fall into the ground and die, it abideth alone: but if it die, it bringeth forth much fruit" Jn. 12: 24.

Jesus used this illustration from nature to point out that, should He preserve His life and be unwilling to die for sinners, He would remain alone and save no one. But by dying on the cross, His life will be fruitful in bringing many sons to glory.

Jesus was celebrated throughout His earthly ministry as He performed miracles, taught with great authority and went about doing good in those days. With all the great results that accompanied His ministry, were it not for God's grace, He simply would have forgotten His

100

primary mission of dying to save humanity. Certain Greeks who were part of a worship service took a bold step after service to insist on having an audience with Jesus. The disciples of Jesus tried to book an appointment for them as requested (Jn. 12: 20-23). At this point Jesus was already engrossed with His primary assignment. In order not to be distracted, when the disciples came to Jesus, He simply answered them and said, the hour has come that the son of man should be glorified. He then followed the sentence up with an explanation: "Except a grain of wheat falls into the ground and dies, it remains as a single grain, but it becomes fruitful when it accepts to be on the ground". This sounds more like a disguised mission statement from the lips of the Master of the Universe.

Like the grain of wheat that must be sacrificed and planted in the ground in order to produce more wheat, so Jesus sacrificed His life, leaving for us an example. According to Rev. A. B. Simpson, "Every true life is death-born, and the deeper the dying the truer the living". If in this life we try to live for ourselves, by pursuing the pleasures of this life at the expense of a sacrificial life of death, then we will set ourselves up for a fall. A true believer must abandon his self-centredness and worldly conformity. He must die to self or else he 'abideth alone'.

Evidence of Crucifixion

"Therefore if you have been raised up with Christ, keep seeking the things above, where Christ is, seated at the right hand of God. Set your mind on the things above, not on the things that are on earth. For you have died and your life is hidden with Christ in God" Col. 3: 1-3 NAS.

The strongest evidence of a crucified life is the change of spiritual taste bud. A young man who used to be a D.J. attended a 'No parking' crusade, organized by Jesus is Life World Outreach Ministry, (a.k.a. JAWOM) in Zaria, Nigeria and gave his life to Christ in a dramatic encounter. The following Sunday he was in Church to testify about the ill-feelings he developed towards worldly music. According to him, he sank all his musical records, numbering over a hundred, in a latrine. With this kind of experience, there is no gain-saying the fact that a change of taste took place in him.

From the above Scriptures, it is clear that there is a need for a shift of focus as evidence of a new life. What this means is that, the mind must disengage from earthly things and re-engage on heavenly things.

The earthly things which tend to engage the mind are such things as money, beauty, prestige, success, fame, power and so on. These are the things that Christians must disengage their minds from. On the other hand, the heavenly things we must engage our minds with include, but not limited to: worship, service to God, sharing the good news, prayer, giving and the likes of such Christian virtues. The true Christian experience gives no room for the flesh to manifest its ugly nature, but propels the believer to stay focused on things above.

A Final Note

The believer is to practice his faith in the world. It would have been a lot easier to live the crucified life, if God had decided to create a new planet for us as soon as we gave our lives to Christ. However, in God's eternal plan, the best place to manifest the crucified life is on planet earth. How then does one navigate through this sinful world without losing his sanctification, so to speak? A new word, sanctification has just been introduced, which typifies the crucified life. To stimulate this lifestyle, the apostle Paul gives us the recipe: *"Finally, brethren, whatsoever things are true, whatsoever things are honest, whatsoever things are just, whatsoever things are pure, whatsoever things are lovely, whatsoever things are of good report; if there by any virtue, and if there be any praise, think on these things"* Phil. 4: 8.

This indeed is a manual handed over to the Philippians by Paul the apostle. The manual contains the list of items to meditate on. He did this to prove the truth that your meditation determines your character. Just as you cannot feed on junk food and expect to live a healthy life, so it is that you cannot ruminate on evil things and expect to live a healthy Christian life. Let every believer work on the list of items enumerated above. This will surely help us to stay within God's boundary.

Chapter Ten

Insist On Faithfulness

ASSUMING A NEW PLANET IS CREATED, called faithfulness and reserved for only those that are faithful. What percentage of the world's current population of over 7 billion people will actually make it to this planet?

The virtue called faithfulness is being eroded by the day. Somehow, as the days go by, we may continue to lose this virtue except a deliberate attempt is made to reverse the trend. One dictionary definition puts faithfulness as being firm in adherence to promises, oaths, contracts, treaties or other engagements. This definition is indicting and calls for a change!

Faithfulness Means Being Loyal

The world would have us think that we don't owe anything to anyone. But to those who have done something for us, sacrificed for us, prayed for us, mentored us, we do owe something: our loyalty. At the time that Elimelech relocated with his wife and two sons to Moab as a result of famine, little did he know that he and his two sons were going to be united in death. It was such a tragic end for three men in one family; and it left behind three widows without their bread winners! The story teaches us that, the mistake of a man could take a great toll on his family.

Well, at the end of the day, the three widows became united in pain. Ruth became an extraordinary daughter-in-law to Naomi (Ruth 1). Her loyalty to her mother-in-law was expressed when she said, *"...Entreat me not to leave thee, or to return from following after thee: for whither thou goest, I will go; and where thou lodgest, I will lodge: thy people shall be my people, and thy God my God: where thou diest, will I die, and there will I be buried: the LORD do so to me, and more also, if aught but death part thee and me."* Ruth 1: 16-17.

This kind of expression of loyalty by Ruth is uncommon. No wonder, God rewarded her loyalty with an uncommon connection with the house of David. She gave birth to the grand father of David the king (Ruth 4: 14-22). And remember, Jesus was the son of David. What a recompense for loyalty!

A look through Scriptures shows that God had always rewarded loyal people. When Elisha was loyal to Elijah, he ended up getting a double portion of Elijah's spirit (2 Kings 2: 1-9). Elisha kept following Elijah from city to city until he got what he was looking for. Loyalty can deliver readily to a man what many days of prayer and fasting attempts to give.

Loyalty is the connection between leadership and the led. It is one of the elements that galvanize the government and the governed together. Each time loyalty is missing, the end product is rebellion. This is what nations are fighting to curb around the world. Believers particularly must remember that we are expected to be loyal to constituted authorities, both within and outside the Church.

Faithfulness means to be Dependable

Would you say it is not right for a man to depend on another man? You may not be far from the truth. By all standards, the most dependable personality is the Almighty, all-knowing, all-wise God. He alone can beat His chest and say, *"And even to your old age, I am he; and even to hoar hairs will I carry you: I have made, and I will bear; even I will carry, and I will deliver you"* (Isaiah 46: 4). When God says I will carry you, it is more than a tranquilizer. All your pains disappear at the point of believing that God is dependable. The greatest wisdom that exists on earth is to learn to depend on God. This is an important lesson to take note of, because the average human being works toward independence. And there is nothing wrong with it, except that it must not include independence from God. To be independent of God is to choose the path of frustration, limitation and regret.

Well, even though man is limited, God still expects that because man was made in His Own image, he should carry a level of dependability. God expects to be able to depend on us. While the unbeliever may not be able to manifest this ability because of the fall of man, it behooves the believer to work on this attribute, because of God's restored image in us at salvation. When Jesus depended on His disciples for prayers in the garden of Gethsemane, they let Him down in that they could not keep a one hour vigil for Him (Matt. 26: 36). But the good news was that Jesus did something to make them dependable before his departure from the world. He told them to tarry in Jerusalem for the Promise of the Father. He assured them that if only the power of God could fall on them, He could entrust them with the assignment of preaching the gospel to the whole world (Acts 1: 4-8). The empowerment from on high made them dependable in passing the gospel with power, from their generation to the next generation. If they had failed, the gospel light would have been quenched. It is my earnest prayer that God will do to us such things that will make us dependable, especially in spiritual assignments.

To a reasonable extent, men should be able to depend on believers. This does not in any way mean believers cannot disappoint people, but it means people can count on Christians often times. There are people that if they tell you they will be visiting your house, you can be sure they won't show up. Believers should not be like them. One of the beauties of Christianity is that it is meant to strengthen relationships. First, relationship with God. Second, relationship with fellow man. And there is no strong relationship outside of dependability of the parties involved. Can a friend count on you when the chips are down? Are you a shoulder for someone to cry on? If you have positive answers to these two questions, then you could be judged dependable.

Without being gender biased, it appears as if women are more dependable in a marriage relationship at difficult moments. A married couple of many years had grown in their love till they became grand parents. One day, the woman fell seriously sick to the point of dying. The man got fed up and abandoned her. But God in His mercy healed the dying woman. Some how, their relationship was restored as a result of God's healing on the woman. Not many years after, the man took ill also. His illness was even worse than the one experienced by his wife some years earlier. Through it all, this woman stood by her husband. By the time the storm was over in the family, the woman who refused to let go her relationship because of a set back became a hero. She was amazingly dependable.

It is so easy a prayer point for people to ask God to surround them with dependable people; but how much do people pray to ask God to make them dependable? In actual sense, the second prayer is far more important. It is like the popular prayer of asking God to send helpers of destiny, yet not being available to help someone else's destiny. What a contradiction!

Faithfulness Means Following God

If you are on twitter, it is normal to receive a request from someone who wants to follow you. If you look at the world of sport, you see that people can get fanatically crazy about a sports man or club. There are those who will tell you they are for Arsenal or Manchester United or some other clubs. They are fans as they would call it. If you ask me to take a position on whether or not it is bad to follow a club, I would rather sit on the fence. This is because, while one cannot categorically say it is wrong, others have followed detrimentally. The so-called 'American idol' has become an idol indeed to some. Other countries have followed suit and now have such things as the 'Nigerian idol' and so on. Some people follow their religion or the doctrine of their religious organization.

The question at this point is, "who or what are you following?" The easiest way to live a wasted life is to follow every other thing or person, except God. David knew this secret so he cried out; *"As the hart panteth after the water brooks, so panted my soul after thee, O God"* (Psalm 42: 1). For David, it was God that unlocked his passion. He was popularly referred to as the man after God's heart. It's a good nickname to bear. If you dared mention God in any matter, David was ready to stake his life. An average Bible student knows that the secret of David was that he was a 'God-chaser'.

The character of the man who wants to follow God must be the desire for the things of God. The term 'desire' is a defining element for people. This is because what you desire determines your direction in life. So, when you see a man who has fixed his desires, he has set a road map for his destiny. When Peter was exhorting a group of young believers, he said to them: *"As newborn babes, desire the sincere milk of the word, that ye may grow thereby"* 1 Pet. 2: 2.

Desire is an important growth factor in the things of God in particular. If our desire for the things of God determines our growth, a continuous desire is needed to sustain our growth. There is no such thing as stunted growth for a believer, except for him that has no desire for the things of God. Similarly, there is no such person as a backslider, except a person that has stopped desiring the things of God. Oh that God will put in the hearts of our youths in this generation, the desire for the things of God! It will be a pleasure to see more youths who are praying for the anointing. It will be wonderful to behold youths who are desirous of God's presence. If young people are addicted to His presence, drug addiction will mean nothing at all to them. This is because the presence of God can deliver far more ecstasy than marijuana or cocaine can do. What can be more satisfying than the fact that, *"...in thy presence is fullness of joy..."* Ps. 16: 11?

God's Commendation

It appears as if man is not actually looking for too many things in life. He is looking for just one thing, and that is the commendation of others. All the fame that people are pursuing is so that they could be commended. All the display of wealth that you see around is actually for commendation. Each time a man succeeds, he expects somebody to pat him on the back. Unfortunately, people are not conscious of God's commendation as much as they are of people's commendation.

A young pastor worked so hard on his message and he delivered it to the congregation with such power. At the end of the service, he waited for people to come around and give him a compliment for a great message, but nobody showed up. He felt bad that his message was not commended, even when he knew that he blessed the congregation of worshipers. Can you see that men want commendation from others? When a sister puts on a new cloth to Church, she expects somebody will make a good comment about it before she leaves Church. If she doesn't get it, she is not made for the day. When my wife makes her hair, she comes back home expecting a comment from me. Of course, I am not good at that. When she fixes a meal, she expects commendation. Certainly, this is an area of strength for me. If we go on and on, you will see that every body wants to be commended. It is actually a basic need for all humans.

For you to know that it is God who actually put the appetite for commendation in man, He also commends people. Often times, people have a wrong picture of God. They think God holds a big stick always wanting to see the next offender that He will use the big stick on. Of course, He does rebuke, but He commends also. If you study the letters to the seven Churches in the book of Revelation, you will see God rebuking them in their areas of weakness and commending them in their areas of strength.

In the parable of the talents in Matt. 25: 14-30, you see Jesus commending two of the servants who did well and rebuking the one who did badly. The interest at this point is on the thing that made Jesus to commend the two servants. This you can see in verses 21 and 23 which are the same in content.

"His lord said unto him, well done, thou good and faithful servant: thou hast been faithful over a few things, I will make thee ruler over many things: enter thou into the joy of thy lord" vs. 21.

The qualities which attracted the Master's comment were 'goodness' and 'faithfulness'. You know what? These two qualities are twin brothers! In God's assessment, 'well done' is more significant than 'long-lived'. May the Lord help the body of Christ to be conscious of the fact that we are living for God's commendation. The whole essence of man's existence on this side of eternity is to be able to earn God's commendation on the last day. Many people pray for long life at the slightest opportunity to do so, without a prayer to earn God's commendation on the last day. But to tell you the truth, there is no greater honour than to live for His commendation. What a happy day it will be, when Jesus gives us a rousing welcome and pat's us on the back, with the words 'well done' proceeding out of His mouth!

The Blessing of Faithfulness

The Scripture is replete with people who were rewarded for faithfulness. When Moses was faithful to God, the Almighty gave him the rare privilege of speaking mouth to mouth with Him. Moses did not only speak with God mouth to mouth, he had a clear revelation of God (Num. 12: 7-8). You will notice that God rose up in defence of him, because of the faithfulness of Moses. Even men can rise up to defend a faithful man in the hour of need, talk less of God. When Daniel was faithful to the assignment of the palace, he became the envy of everybody. His faithfulness actually earned him a place in the heart of the king, as well as promotion in his place of work (Dan. 6: 1-4).

When God found Timothy faithful, He placed him in the ministry (1 Tim. 1: 12). The formula of God in all generations is that, before He uses man in a great way, He tests him in small ways. The marking scheme for His tests is 'faithfulness'. Here is a Scriptural question to ponder on: *"And if ye have not been faithful in that which is another man's, who shall give you that which is your own?* Luke 16: 12.

There is no great man in the sight of God that was not first a faithful man. Throughout the Bible, faithfulness eclipses fame as a mark of greatness. As men remain faithful to His call on their lives, He comes around to bless them from time to time. This understanding should help us stay focused in the things that God expects us to do. The Bible says, *"A faithful man shall abound with blessings..."* Prov. 28: 20. Just to capture all that have been said about the blessing of faithfulness in one sentence, here it goes: God's approach to life is that He rewards faithfulness with fruitfulness.

Chapter Eleven

The White Garment

THE CHURCH SEEMS TO HAVE LOST some grounds on the subject of righteousness and holiness. But this ought to be the core of Christianity after salvation. The primary purpose why Jesus had to sacrifice so much to the point of giving Himself for the Church is: *"That he might sanctify and cleanse it with the washing of water by the word, That he might present it to himself a glorious church, not having spot, or wrinkle, or any such thing; but that it should be holy and without blemish"* Eph. 5: 26-27.

Righteousness and holiness are twin characters that every believer should be adorned with. These two characters are closely related, but they have a dividing line. Not to dwell too much on theological explanation for these two virtues, a statement from the mouth of Jesus could be used to differentiate between righteousness and holiness.

At one time that Jesus was faced with the hypocrisy of the Pharisees, He had no option than to tell them exactly their state:*"...For you clean the outside of the cup and of the dish, but inside they are full of robbery and self-indulgence"* (Matt. 23: 25 NAS). What is the analogy? Holiness could be likened to the inside of the cup being clean, whereas righteousness could be likened to the outside of the cup being clean. The two are needed for a great Christian experience. Holiness is God's nature in us. It is called the seed of God and when it abides in us, we cannot make sin a practice. Since the Bible says, our righteousness is like filthy rags before Him (Isaiah 64: 6), it means we need something more than 'self-righteousness' and so Jesus became our righteousness (1 Cor. 1: 30), so that we can become the righteousness of God in Christ Jesus.

It was David who asked a question in Ps. 24: 3, about the qualification of he that can stand in the holy place of the Lord and he provided the answer in the next verse: *"He that hath clean hands and a pure heart..."* vs. 4. 'Clean hands' as stated here has to do with righteousness, whereas 'pure heart' has to do with holiness. So, it can be said that a man with clean hands is righteous, whereas a man with a pure heart is holy. This is corroborated in Scripture that says: *"Blessed are the pure in heart: for they shall see God"* Matt. 5: 8 and the one that says: *"...and holiness, without which no man shall see the Lord"* Heb 12: 14. Purity of heart or holiness is the qualification needed in order to see the Lord.

No matter the evil we committed before we gave our lives to Christ, at the point of salvation, His righteousness declared us 'not guilty'. In God's salvation package, the righteousness of Christ deletes a man's wrong doings when he confesses Christ as his Saviour. After a man is declared righteous because of the shed blood of Christ on the cross of Calvary, God puts His nature in him so as to enable him to love righteousness as a way of life. That nature of God implanted in us to enable us live right, is what holiness is about.

The Nature of God

The holiness of God is what makes Him distinct from all other deities. There is no deity that has claimed to be holy apart from the God of Heaven. He says, "...*Ye shall therefore be holy, for I am holy*" Lev. 11: 45. It is in the fact that God is holy, that we are inspired towards holiness. As a matter of fact, the angels of God in Heaven have beheld so much of God's holy nature to the point that their cry reflects it. In Isaiah 6: 3, the Bible records; "*And one cried unto another, and said, Holy, holy, holy, is the LORD of hosts: the whole earth is full of his glory.*"

According to Sproul, "When the Bible calls God holy, it means primarily that God is transcendentally separate. He is so far above and beyond us that He seems almost totally foreign to us". That is to say, He is in a different class from us in terms of His nature. Two Scriptural quotations can substantiate the above statement.

"Who is like unto thee, O LORD, among the gods? Who is like thee, glorious in holiness, fearful in praises, doing wonders?" Exodus 15: 11.

"There is none holy as the LORD: for there is none beside thee: neither is there any rock like our God" I Sam. 2: 2.

Based on these two Scriptures, ladies and gentlemen, it is safe to conclude that when it comes to the issue of holiness, God has no rival. A vision of this holy God gives us a photograph of our sinful nature. That was what made Isaiah to cry woe is me! (Isaiah 6: 5). The good news is that each time we cry out to God about our sinful nature, He performs a spiritual surgery that leaves us healthier at the end. The prophet Isaiah experienced this kind of surgery and as such, his life did not end in a lamentation.

A Look at the Ten Commandments

When God gave the Ten Commandments to Israel and by extension to all of mankind, He did that so as to establish a good relationship among people. The relationship which He sought to establish at that time was two dimensional: relationship with God and with others. Though, the first and most important relationship is the relationship with God. In trying to communicate this, the first four commandments concentrated on relationship with God. Of course, the last six dealt extensively on relationship with others. These two types of relationships are what spiritual experts call the vertical and horizontal relationships.

The vertical relationship has to do with God and the horizontal relationship deals with fellow man.

In actual sense, when your relationship with God is good, you will have a cordial relationship with others. Even if you have enemies that are known to you, the fact that you have a good relationship with God will help you to relate well with them. A difficult but not an impossible task which God has given to us is: *"Follow peace with all men, and holiness, without which no man shall see the Lord"* Heb. 12: 14.

The first four commandments that God gave to Israel was supposed to produce holiness in the people, whereas the last six of the Ten Commandments was supposed to engender righteousness. So, it could be said that holiness is vertical and righteousness is horizontal as far as the two aforementioned relationships are concerned. In the words of one man of God, holiness is spiritual, whereas righteousness is practical. These two are important and we must take responsibility for them. In Ephesians 4: 24 the Bible tells us our responsibility in this regard: *"And that ye put on the new man, which after God is created in righteousness and true holiness"*.

The new man as referred to in Scriptures, talks about our new life in Christ. This new life in Christ is not about reformation, it is rather about transformation. When a man gives his life to Christ, a spiritual transaction takes place leading to a change of heart. This transaction produces an entirely new spiritual outlook and this is what is called transformation. It is the transformed life and not the reformed life that wins in the face of temptation.

Well, the Ten Commandments could not achieve the dual purpose of producing holiness and righteousness in the people of God. In actual sense, there were several other laws that came into existence in God's dealings with His people. On a sad note however, none of these laws could achieve much because of the inherent weaknesses in both man and in the external laws. God then promised He would write His laws in the heart of man (Jer. 31: 33-34). Obviously, what man needed were God's laws internalized. This was achieved by the shed blood of Jesus on the cross of Calvary (Heb. 10: 16-26). Thank God that the failure of the Ten Commandments was not the end to the search for holiness and righteousness.

Clearly, it has been shown from the discussion that the two terms; holiness and righteousness have a dividing line. Even from the Greek word for each of them the difference can be spotted. The Greek word for holiness is 'hagiasmos' which denotes a moral nature in pursuit of God's likeness. The Greek word for righteousness is 'dikaiosune' and it means to deal justly and honestly with others. Though these two terms are not equal in meaning, there is nothing wrong in using them interchangeably, so long as it conveys the primary message of being right with God, as often used in the Christian circle.

The Call

"Let thy garments be always white; and let thy head lack no ointment" Eccl. 9: 8.

Because of the reality that we are in constant touch with the world, which is a dusty environment, there exists a possibility of soiling our garments. Take for example, the fact that we live in a fast paced world, where everybody is in a hurry to make it. A believer could be tempted to go the way of the world as he rushes to meet up with certain obligations. In the process he could get his garment soiled. By the way, impatience is one of the things that could lead people into sin. Often times, when people feel pained over what God has not yet done as at when expected, they tend to forget that God has His eyes on the big picture.

The call here is that no matter what happens, a believer must ensure that his garment is always white. The onus is actually on the believer. Nevertheless, the believer is not alone in the business of keeping his garment white. God has made the necessary provision so that this requirement may be possible. The blood is God's provision for a white garment. The blood of Jesus is the divine detergent that could be used by the believer, each time there is an awareness of a dirty garment. First, the sin must be confessed, and then the application of the cleansing blood follows. This step is properly captured in 1 Jn. 1: 9; *"If we confess our sins, he is faithful and just to forgive us our sins, and to cleanse us from all unrighteousness"*.

Chapter Twelve

Catch the Fire

A QUICK LOOK THROUGH SCRIPTURES REVEALS several prophets that God used to the glory of His name. All of these biblical prophets were unique in one way or the other. One of these prophets, popularly called the weeping prophet by Bible scholars was Jeremiah. This prophet was in a class of his own, because of the measure of fire that he carried in his bones.

"Then I said, I will not make mention of him, nor speak any more in his name. But his word was in mine heart as a burning fire shut up in my bones, and I was weary with forbearing, and I could not stay" Jer. 20: 9.

In concluding this book, I like to say that the believer who wants to make it to Heaven in this end time must carry a 'threshold' level of fire. As the battle gets fiercer, the fire of God in our bones becomes much more needed. Here is an alarm: "there is a thick darkness that has covered people, and this darkness is encroaching on the believers, only a people of fire can resist it."

Because Jeremiah carried fire in his bones, he could not hold back what God had put in his heart. When there is a fire in a man's bones, it becomes impossible to hold back what God has put in his heart. As I began to write on this subject of fire in my bones', it became evidently clear to me that one reason why many believers are docile and they take the back seat in the things of God is because there is lack of fire in their bones. Lack of fire is a disease of the end time Church that needs to be addressed quickly.

It is a thing of concern that some believers that used to be carriers of fire many years back have lost some heat. Loss of fire is a big loss that should make believers cry out to God until it is restored. The truth is God would rather have you cold than lukewarm.

"So then because thou art lukewarm, and neither cold nor hot, I will spew thee out of my mouth" Rev. 3: 16.

Can you see that God is not comfortable with the state of a lukewarm person? The greatest prayer of all time is to ask God for a revival that rekindles His fire in your life.

Indications of Fire

The background story of Jeremiah 20: 9 was that, in the course of the prophet's assignment, he got into trouble.

Pashur the son of Immer the priest, who was also chief governor in the house of the Lord, smote Jeremiah and locked him up for prophesying in the name of the Lord. Jeremiah got so disturbed by the ill treatment which he received, to the point that he resigned from the ministry in his heart.

"Then I said, I will not make mention of him, nor speak any more in his name..." Jer. 20: 9.

Some how, because of the fire that the prophet carried, he could not make good his promise to quit the job. There is no believer who carries fire that resigns from his God-given assignment, no matter the offence. When you see a believer who suddenly says he is no longer interested in what he is doing for God, it is an indication of a dying fire.

When a man carries fire he stands up for Jesus. Of course, it takes courage to stand up for Jesus in the face of opposition. But the fire that we carry delivers unto us the needed courage each time. The disciples of Jesus carried so much fire to the extent that the threat of being beaten by the enemies of the gospel could not deter them from preaching the gospel (Acts 5: 18-42).

Hear the answer which the men who carried fire gave in reply to the opposition that they faced: *"For we cannot but speak the things which we have seen and heard"* Acts 4: 20. If a man cannot stand up for Jesus, he is not man enough.

There is a story in Scripture about a man that I love so much. This man by name Phinehas was so zealous and was courageous enough to stand up for Jesus in a crisis situation.

"And when Phinehas, the son of Eleazar, the son of Aaron the priest, saw it, he rose up from among the congregation, and took a javelin in his hand;

And he went after the man of Israel into the tent, and thrust both of them through, the man of Israel, and the woman through her belly. So the plague was stayed from the children of Israel" Num. 25: 7-8.

There was trouble in Israel because the Israelites began to commit sexual immorality with the daughters of Moab and Israel worshiped their gods. With these behaviours, the Almighty was angry and He responded with judgment to the people. At this point, a young man that was not sober at the Lord's judgment brought his girl friend to public glare in order to catch some fun. But glory to God, there was another young man who had fire in his bones and will not watch an abomination go on in the name of what is in vogue. He stood up and confronted the evil of his time that was ravaging the people. In this generation, the word of God is the sword with which to confront the evil of our time. A believer who carries fire has a mandate to confront the evil of his generation. This he does by living in the truth, preaching the truth and insisting on the truth of God's word.

To a great extent, the analysis of the life of David shows he was a man who carried fire. He was sent by his father to go and see how his brothers were doing on the field. When he got there, he met the people of God being challenged by Goliath of Gath. Each time this giant showed up, the Israelites went into hiding. This scenario made David angry and he decided to do something about it. To say it point blank, the reason why an army of God will go into hiding at the sight of Goliath is as a result of a lack of fire.

When the man who carried fire, in the person of David came, Goliath knew the difference. The fire that burned within David did not allow him to watch the people of God being harassed by the enemy (1 Sam. 17: 9-24). The concern of David was: *"...for who is this uncircumcised Philistine, that he should defy the armies of the living God?"* Vs. 26. The secret of David in confronting Goliath was that he had a measure of fire. When a man carries fire, he stops at nothing until Goliath's head is brought down.

The Need for Fire

The need for fire in the life of a believer cannot be over emphasized. It is the burning fire that makes us to shine. The Bible says, John was a burning and a shining light (Jn. 5: 35). It is a burning fire that makes for a shining light. Know for sure that how bright you are able to shine, is determined by how intense you are able to burn. A lot of believers want to shine in life, but the question is, are they ready to burn? Because of the fact that David carried fire, he had a singular quest: *"AS THE hart panteth after the water brooks, so panteth my soul after thee, O God"* Ps. 42: 1.

When a man longs for God he is actually burning for the Lord. The question is where is your passion? A correct answer to this question will tell whether or not you carry fire. Some people have their passion in fashion. Such people can tell you the latest in the world of fashion, but if you ask them to pray for five minutes, they start yawning. That indeed is lack of fire. Others could watch movies for hours but they cannot be in a Church service for three hours. It is a lack of fire for our Churches to be filled with people in a Sunday service and nearly empty during the week. Attending Church once a week makes for a fireless Christian. Oh! God put some fire in our bones that this generation may burn and do exploits for you!

Igniting the Fire

The apostle Paul, writing to the Roman Church admonishes them thus: *"Not slothful in business, fervent in spirit, serving the Lord"* Rom. 12: 11. The only way not to be slothful in business is to be fervent in spirit. And fervency of spirit could be properly tagged as fire in action. Friend, make up your mind not to be slothful in the Lord's business. In addition to that, the Lord requires and charges us to pay attention to prayers. Each time you pray, you leave behind an impact of fire in your bones.

Of course, there is no fire without the word. When you sit with the word of God, you add fire to your life. Jeremiah said: "...*But his word was in mine heart as a burning fire shut up in my bones....*" Jer. 20: 9.

Let your heart retain His words and don't let the cares of this life choke the word out of your life. When Martha could not make provision for the word in her life, Jesus rebuked her for it. At the time Jesus visited the two sisters, Martha and Mary, they took Him in. Obviously, Martha was excited at the visit of Jesus and she quickly tried to serve Him some refreshment. Mary probably was also excited, but she was more attracted to Him and that made her to sit at His feet to learn of Him. The difference between the two sisters was that while Martha was excited about the Master's visit, Mary was attracted to His visit. To Mary, the coming of Jesus was so magnetic that she could not leave His presence for a minute. The question is, are you attracted to Jesus or you are only excited about Him?

While Jesus rebuked Martha for being cumbered by much serving, He commended Mary for choosing the good part (Luke. 10: 38-42). What was the good part that Mary chose? The choice to sit with the word was the good part.

God asked a question in Jeremiah 23: 29; "*Is not my word like as a fire? Saith the Lord...*" The answer is yes His word is fire. The rule of thumb is that each time you add His word to your life you increase the fire, and each time you preach the word, you spread the fire. And the wisdom is that we need both to increase and to spread the fire. The final part of this book is a prayer that God will not let our love for Him to grow cold and that wherever there is a burning out of the fire of God He will light the fire again!

One More Word

In His secret discussion with Nicodemus, Jesus made a profound statement that should be taken seriously by every living soul: "... *Verily, verily, I say unto thee, Except a man be born again, he cannot see the kingdom of God*" Jn. 3: 3.

No matter how long a man lives on earth, one day he will eventually die. His life after death will then be determined by how he lived his life on earth. If he was born again and lived for Christ, he spends his eternity in Heaven. Otherwise, the miserable side of eternity, that is, hell becomes his abode.

In order to have Jesus come into your life and be born again, you should take the following steps:

1. Acknowledge that you are a sinner (Rom. 3: 23)

2. Acknowledge that you need a Saviour (Jn. 3: 16).

3. Repent of your sins (Luke 15: 10)

4. Believe in the Lord Jesus in your heart and confess it with your mouth (Rom. 10: 9-10).

Now, say this prayer genuinely from you heart. Dear Jesus, I recognize that I am a sinner. I repent of my sins today. Come into my life right now and cleanse me from all my sins. Give me the power to live a changed life from this day forward. Thank You for accepting me as Your child. Amen.